This book is extremely valuable to read. It demonstrates how to go from status quo to creating a winning future success. Her thoughts are not only original but practical as well. Very timely for today's market.

—**JERRY R. MITCHELL,** Serial Entrepreneur, Forbes 1997

Jackie is a miracle; you will gain more than you can imagine in this power packed book!

—**SARAH VICTORY,** Author of Double Your Business in One Year or Less

Jackie Camacho-Ruiz's The Little Book of Business Secrets That Work! is a must read for anyone that wants to start a business or is in business!

—**MICHELE ARDEN,** President Arden & Associates

After 45 years in the Marketing - Advertising - Promotion business I sometimes feel jaded. As much as I enjoy the business, a person has come along that has heightened my enjoyment in marketing just that much more - Jackie CR. I was hard pressed to think of an appropriate word to describe her. That word is VERVE! (V) Vivacity, (E) Energetic, (R) Responsive, (V) full of Vigor, (E) Enthusiastic.

—**J. FREDERICK BAKER,** Bakers Marketing Group

THE LITTLE BOOK OF BUSINESS SECRETS that work!

200 How-To's Every Business Professional Needs to Know

JACQUELINE CAMACHO-RUIZ

The Little Book of Business Secrets That Work!

Edited by Vicki Martinka Petersen and Corey Michael Blake.

Disclaimer:
All information depicted in "The Little Book of Business Secrets That Work!" is based on the life experiences of the author, Jacqueline Camacho-Ruiz, and is solely based on her recollection of those experiences.

www.bizsecretsthatwork.com
www.writersoftheroundtable.com
Cover design and layout by Juan Pablo Ruiz,
JJR Marketing Consultants, LLC.

Printed and bound in the U.S.A.

ISBN: 9780982220696

Library of Congress Control Number: 2010927514

How to use this book

Open up the book on any page
or go to a specific section.

Apply the secret exercise.

Share with somebody else.

Make it happen today!

*This book is not intended to replace professional advice. Knowledge provided in this book is based on experiences that have proven successful for the author. Results may vary. Not every secret is for everyone.

Contents:

Section 1 - Start Ups

Section 2 - Sales

Section 3 - Marketing

Section 4 - Customer Retention

Section 5 - Motivation

Acknowledgements

Success cannot be achieved without the support of those that love you. First and foremost, I would like to thank my husband, Juan Pablo, for his tenacious support throughout the process. Also, I greatly appreciate my children, Leonardo and Giulianna, for being the driving force that keeps me going. Special thanks to my mother and father for igniting the burning desire in me since my childhood, and to my brothers, Efrain and Salvador, for their constant support.

Thanks to all my mentors for constantly believing in me, especially Clark Weber, who inspired me to begin journaling about my business life. Also, special thanks to my Mastermind partner Chris Beebe for inspiring me to make this happen. Thanks to Greg Sigerson, for his constant support and for waking up so early everyday to patiently interview me, brainstorm, simplify and polish these secrets. Thanks to Michele Kelly for capturing the essence of this book in the introduction.

I am very grateful to Luanne Mayorga, Cher Garrett, Mary Erlain, Ray Stuckly, Michael Machado, Mario Ponce, Rogerio Charu, Michele Arden, Marlene Baczek, Heather Ruiz, Jim Kendall, Jerry Mitchell, Russ Riendeau, Sarah Victory, Irene Anzola, Trey Morris, Robert Renteria, Sharon Eckart, Ed Horn, Brian Marshall among many others who have touched my life. For those of you whose names I did not mention, you know who you are.

Thank you!

—JACQUELINE CAMACHO-RUIZ

Foreword

My job as a former radio personality, author, and president of an advertising agency looks glamorous, and it's not uncommon for some people to want to emulate it. When told what the road involves, almost all take a pass with one or two exceptions. In December of 2005, I met a bright, wide-eyed, and charming young lady who is the author of this book, Jackie Camacho-Ruiz. She looked me in the eye and said she wanted to develop her own advertising agency. This book, "The Little Book of Business Secrets That Work!" is the result of her journey. Don't just read it, etch it in your heart, and you'll also enjoy the kind of success that Jackie enjoys. Do it! Success is the child of audacity!

—CLARK WEBER
Radio Celebrity - Clark Weber Associates

Introduction

A CHANCE CONVERSATION. THAT'S ALL IT WAS.

Maybe you're just starting out. Maybe you're a business veteran. Either way, we all need inspiration from which to innovate our companies and organizations. And, being true to myself, this meant that I could no longer keep these words—mined from numerous conversations with top business experts, mentors, and my own personal experiences to myself. I was driven to share them in the hopes that they would prove to be authentic, applicable, usable lessons for others to climb their own business mountains and succeed.

I was being interviewed for a story on entrepreneurship by Clark Weber, a renowned national radio host. Somewhere amidst our conversation, he suggested I write about the journey of my business. The word just clicked. My journey – that was a perfect word to describe this amazing path my life had taken as the Make-it-Happen Director for an award-winning marketing agency. I started writing on January 15, 2008, and, 276 business lessons later, Diary of a Young, Successful Entrepreneur was born.

Honestly, my intention was never to write a book. But after hundreds of conversations with clients and industry peers, I began to realize that this journal resonated with wisdom that could touch the lives of many people.

Even before I took pen to paper, my journey began with a passion for learning, sharing, and helping others. Born in Mexico City, I came to the United States when I was 14 years old, learning English in one year, attending college, and blazing a trail for helping companies grow their businesses through integrated marketing.

That's why I want to share this book with you.

So, as you turn these pages, please know that there are many of us walking by your side. Yes, we are there, whispering words born from our successes as well as our failures, crafted from our best days in business and inspired by our greatest challenges.

My journey? Now, it is yours, too.

—JACQUELINE CAMACHO-RUIZ

Section 1
Start Ups

Starting a business is difficult. As a young entrepreneur, I have learned quite a few lessons that I want to share with you. The following secrets will help you navigate the world of business as an entrepreneur. You are not alone!

It takes a special person to be an entrepreneur

By definition, an entrepreneur is a person who possesses a new enterprise, venture, or idea and assumes significant accountability for the inherent risks and outcome. In other words, being an entrepreneur means having the guts to follow your dream regardless of what people say. It means leaving the comfort of a guaranteed paycheck and risking it all. It is about following your passion, being a leader and making your vision a reality through creativity and belief.

When I embarked on this journey of entrepreneurship a few years ago, many people were against it. I was a very young woman who had just given birth to my first child. I remember how difficult it was to make people believe in me, and the odds of success seemed against me. All I wanted was to serve businesses and truly redefine marketing. I knew that I wanted to make a difference in the marketplace—that my heart was there and that failure was not an option. I began investing my time, resources, and energy into this business idea.

After a few years, entrepreneurship has been an amazing journey with a trail of success and incredible rewards for me and my family. Entrepreneurship can help you fulfill your passion and create unimaginable success!

Are you ready to embark on this journey?
Check the boxes below if you have what it takes:

☐ Competency
☐ Viable business concept
☐ Access to adequate capital

If you have the three elements above, you are at the right place at the right time!

Success begins in your mind

Whatever your mind can conceive, you can achieve. To create something physical in your life, you must believe it first because that is the only way that it is going to show up. If you believe in it, it is yours. For example, saying, "I want to be on TV," seems like a huge vision for most people. If I say to people, "I am going to be on TV next year," people might laugh at me and say, "TV is for celebrities, are you crazy ... are you nuts?" But, if I can play that in my mind, I know it will happen. The power of recognizing something and playing it in your mind is so huge that if you are able to do it, you can consider it done. When you see it and believe it, you're going to be more prone to act on it, and we need to connect those two lines.

Identify one goal:

____

____

____

____

Visualize the end result in your mind at least once a day.

Find and follow your passion

What is it you have always wanted to do? What is your mission in this world? You might not have the answers. You might not have found yet your passion – the thing you truly love to do that makes you excited and motivated. The good news is you can find your passion and motivation because the answers are inside of you. Ask yourself what you want, and make it happen. Be persistent in looking for this.

When I was about 16 years old, I did not know what my passion was. In fact, I had more questions than answers. Recently, my mother, who now resides in Mexico, read a letter that I wrote to myself at about that age. The letter contained not answers, but several questions about my life. I was asking myself why and how I could find my true passion. Now, a few years later, I have found the answers to most of those questions, but most importantly, I have found my true passion. If you don't know what your passion is, be inquisitive; ask questions.

Have you found your passion?
If not, write three questions below to help you find your passion:

____

____

____

____

The answers will be revealed to you.

Passion has no language; it comes from the heart!

Visit **www.bizsecretsthatwork.com/questions.pdf** to see the original questions I asked myself (in Spanish).

Put yourself first

As you begin a business, it is very easy to put yourself last—last to get the benefits of your enterprise, last to get paid. According to Scott Sinclair, a successful entrepreneur for over 12 years, he learned this lesson the hard way. "You can't start a business by making everybody happy. You can't be the nice guy all the time. It is important to implement policies and procedures to follow so that you stay focused and your team stays focused as well."

Be aware that your employees can have a portion of your vision, but they will never have the entire vision simply because they are not you. As you navigate this journey, recognize and get the right people on board to help you carry out small parts of your vision based on their expertise. For example, one employee can handle all the administrative tasks, another can handle the finances, and you can be in charge of business development. Now, with these individuals on board, it is easier to carry out your vision of success.

What is your vision statement as a business owner?

____

____

____

____

Identify three people who can help you carry out that vision:

1_______________________________________

2_______________________________________

3_______________________________________

005

Define the things that you naturally do well

This means defining the things that come naturally to you—those things that you do well and that you don't need to invest much energy into. Assessing the talents and skills that make you unique and give you a natural competency allows you to help other people. If you can tap into what you do well and share that with other people, the quality of the product you can bring to the marketplace will be superior to your competitors.

Focus on bringing solutions to your clients, and bring the strategy they need to improve their business. I tap into other people who I know do things well in areas where I don't excel. By recognizing what you do well and not investing your energy into those things you don't do well naturally, you really get the best of all worlds. You get top talent in other fields, and you create a team effort.

Create a list of things you naturally do well:

____

____

____

____

How can you apply those gifts to affect your bottom line?

____

____

____

____

Consciously use them this week.

Assessing the talents and skills that make you unique gives you a natural competency that allows you to help others.

Stay true to yourself and believe

It's all about authenticity and not bending your integrity to accommodate a situation. It means knowing you are built with an inner guidance system. It also means every answer that you seek - in business, personally, professionally, spiritually, emotionally - is inside of you. Every single one.

Really, every answer you've ever sought is inside of you. The solutions you seek are in your mind, in your heart, in your subconscious mind, through the power of the universe and the power of that superior force that moves us. And when you know that, that is all you need. Listen to your inner guidance to achieve that dream. Through those feelings, you will know if you are staying true to yourself or not. If something doesn't make you feel good, it is probably not the right thing to do.

Being authentic and being true to yourself is never easy. In a given situation, listen to your intuition. Become aware that you have it. For some people who are very logically minded, just acknowledging that they have intuition is a huge leap.

Listen. What exactly are you feeling? Become aware of your feelings. Next, take an action on those feelings. What action can you take today based on your feelings?

____

____

____

____

____

007

Stay true to the foundation of your business

This does not mean that your business should not evolve or change according to the trends in the marketplace. This means you should look back and ask, "Why did I start the business? Was it because I want to make a difference in the world? Was it because I am invigorated by helping people? What is it that makes me get up every morning?"

I wanted to make a difference in business. Think about why you exist as a company. If you can stay true to the foundation of your business, you will be successful no matter what. If that foundation is sustainable, you will be successful.

What is the foundation of your business?

____

____

____

____

____

Define your areas of opportunity

What can we do with the things we have now? There are many areas of your business that you have not capitalized on, whether it is tapping into a new market or getting an expert on your team. You must be open and define where you can take your business. What are your opportunities, and how can you maximize them? Remember to always look for and create new opportunities. Streamline the process, and provide savings in that process to your clients, which will result in them being happy.

Step away from your desk for a night or a weekend, and look at your business objectively.

Ask yourself how you can maximize those opportunities. What step will you take today?

____

____

____

____

Visit **www.bizsecretsthatwork.com/swot** to download a free copy of Strengths, Weaknesses, Opportunities, and Threats (SWOT) analysis exercise.

Create value from nothing

When you expand on something that already exists, it is nothing new. But when you create a formula and a process, then you are creating value. Create your standards and formulas. Your unique experiences and talents can create something that has never existed before. You are creating a new category—a situation where you have no competition. We all want to be in that place where we are the only ones capable of doing something. Creating something new requires you to really look at your talents, motivations, and strenghts. Take those and combine them into something completely unique and completely you. As you do this, you will find people who are looking for exactly that value you bring to the table. Find your own uniqueness, and align it with your determined purpose. This creates that passion, that enthusiasm, that excitement—all the things that generate business and move people through. It is not a small process, but it is worth exploring.

Take a strength assessment.

How can this strength be of value to someone else?

___

___

___

___

This provides you with the opportunity to create that arbitrage, that value from nothing.

Align yourself with mentors

It's impossible to know everything there is to know. We all need to learn new skills. Aligning yourself with people who are smarter and more experienced than you are can really put you ahead of the game. You see, everything we will ever accomplish will be with people, through people, and for people. By far, aligning yourself with people is one of the most incredible things you can do. Why not choose the best of the best to help you achieve your goals?

Who do you consider your three main mentors, and what will you do to get their support this week?

1. ______________________________
2. ______________________________
3. ______________________________

If you don't have a mentor, what will you do to find one and get their support?

____

____

____

____

011

Recognize when you need help

We think we can do it all like we're superheroes. The problem is, we are not. When things get out of hand, we have to recognize that we need help. Select carefully who you ask for help. It must be someone you can trust deeply. You might need a different perspective from someone else, and you'll need to recognize and accept that help.

Discipline is very important. You must have self-discipline to complete your tasks. You can accomplish things you did not think you could by seeking help! You can build relationships and achieve happiness.

Define one area you need help with:

____

____

____

Ask for help and accept it!

Get the right people on board

There are ways to fill your life and work with positive energy. You must give your teams and subcontractors a vision of accomplishments. Whatever your visions for your business or your life, they should be aligned with people who are in the same situation you are in. What is your methodology? What are your core values? These are what you look for in your team. Create your energy with those around you.

Identify one project wich you're working on.

____

____

Identify three people who can help you accomplish this.

1. ____________________________________
2. ____________________________________
3. ____________________________________

013

Have a good team of professionals by your side

Surrounding yourself with top-notch people is important because so many people make so many mistakes starting out. They go into business because they know what they do best. They know that they are a great carpenter or a great restaurateur; but they don't know the minutiae that go along with running the business. They don't know the legalities or the accounting responsibilities of having a business. They don't know which licenses they need to get. They might not even know the operations side. But having a good team of professionals by your side from the beginning, and allowing the budget to cover those initial expenses, can save you so many headaches. It can really streamline the process and get you up and running quicker than you think. The money you spend, instead of doing it yourself, will be money well spent.

Having an expert in every area of your business can save you time and energy, and propel you to success in a much shorter period of time. It's better than going with trial and error.

If you are thinking about starting a business, please identify the following:

Accountant: ____________________________________

Attorney: ____________________________________

Insurance broker: ____________________________________

Marketer: ____________________________________

Reserve your trust

We want to believe everyone is good and nobody is bad. But rely on your feelings to let you know if you should trust a person or not. You have to reflect your own vibes onto the people you want to work with, and feelings are a great rating system that helps you identify those who are worthy of your trust.

Monitor how you feel when you meet people. What vibes are you picking up?

Be aware of those feelings, and make the choice not to associate with people if you don't get good vibes.

Encourage your team

When your team feels demoralized and unappreciated, they will not be motivated to work to their fullest capacity. Let your team know what you expect from them and what the goals are. Let them know the objectives and mission for the company and give your team the opportunity to execute them. Evaluate your team to see if they are producing tangible results. Then praise them and recognize that they did a good job. Employees should be motivated and inspired to do more for the company; everybody wants to feel important. If you make people feel important, you will have a much more productive team.

Apply the following four-step process with your team:

1. *Let employees know the expectations.*
2. *Give them opportunities.*
3. *Evaluate them.*
4. *Praise them or repeat the first step.*

Stay ahead of the game with action items

We all have a lot of things to do, both personally and professionally. One of the biggest challenges entrepreneurs face is the anxiety that comes with all the hats we wear. As a wife, mother, entrepreneur, speaker, and author, life gets very busy for me at times. The way I stay ahead is by creating an ongoing list of action items. Nothing feels better to me than scratching off an item completed on my list. It's critical to be proactive and to anticipate and complete action items. To manage the ever growing list of action items, follow the exercise below.

Look at the list below carefully.

- ~~*Go grocery shopping*~~
- *Organize office*
- *Send presentation to clients*

Do you feel the responsibility to complete those items that are not crossed off and a sense of relief for those that are completed?

Now write your own list of action items for today:

____

____

____

____

____

Writing your own lists will ensure that you stay ahead of the game.

Know what your time is worth

Your billable hours are usually one-third of the total time spent working. The other two-thirds go to business development and administrative efforts. For example, if you want to make $50,000, you must divide it into 52 weeks, which comes out to $961 per week. Now you take that number and divide it by how many hours you want to work per week, for example, if you want to work 40 hours per week, you need to make $24 per hour. Considering, however, that only one-third of your hours are billable (because you'll be busy performing tasks that aren't generating revenue), you would either have to work 120 hours per week or charge $72 per hour based on weekly billable hours of 13.3.

How much do you want to make this year?

Apply this formula:

$______________ per year / 52 weeks= $______________

$______________ per week/ _______________hours per week=

$______________ hourly rate

Do you change the number of hours you work or the amount you charge per hour?

If you adjust the amount of hours you work or amount you charge per hour, you will earn what you want to this year!

018

See the value of charging for your services

Sometimes we are scared about charging when we don't know the impact that we can make for a business. You may think you do not deserve to get paid or that you do not deserve the amount you are charging. Start-up businesses struggle with this: How do I charge? Is this a fair value? You need to recognize the value of charging for your services. You must close your eyes and think of the impact that you make in the world with your services. How does your business being in the world make a difference? Maybe it's a small thing or maybe it's in the way you deliver your products or services.

Write down three things that are of value to the relationship you have with your clients. What services can you offer that nobody else can match?

1. ______________________________
2. ______________________________
3. ______________________________

019

Charge accordingly

You must charge according to the services you deliver; do not lower your price according to what the client is willing to pay. If you are going to compromise, do so in a way that if your client is going to pay you less than what you quoted then you are going to do less.

Every client has different needs, and based on those needs, requirements, and the time investment, it is important to provide a service they appreciate because they are paying for that service. You will be satisfied that you are not being taken advantage of because you are giving the value to the client that they deserve and vice versa. You create a win-win situation. You need to charge appropiately because it is not fair to your other clients who are currently paying the going rate. It is also not fair to your family because they are not receiving the income you are capable of providing, and it is not fair to you.

You are providing a service. Your clients are paying for the time that it takes to complete the job, and for your expertise.

In the process of a negotiation, when somebody says, "I can't afford that," readjust the price, but also readjust the product so that it is equitable.

If clients want to take away money, you have to take away services. If clients want to add money you have to add services.

Don't be afraid of making money

Pursuing your passion means being paid to do what you love, so don't be afraid to take money for it. As an entrepreneur, you are creating everything from scratch. Think about all the effort that you put into things. You deserve the money that you are making, even if it is not much yet. If you are not intimidated and you are confident, it's going to be easier for you to grow and move to the next level.

Make a list of three of your most profitable clients - the clients bringing in the most money:

____

____

____

Write down the reasons you deserve their money: what have you done for them?

____

____

____

You deserve the money you earn!

Bring businesses together (strategic alliances)

The value you create by doing this for your clients is incredible. You might bring businesses together that are not necessarily in the same industry or the same *vertical.* This can be done by going out of your way to make an introduction or connection that could possibly turn into something amazing for them and, in return, for you. For example, I discovered a client needed financial services. As a marketing agency, I have nothing to do with financial services, but I always try to see if I can find a resource for a client. This effort, in exchange, adds value to what I'm doing as a business. Indirectly, it brings a tremendous amount of value to me with clients saying, "You didn't have to do this, but you went out of your way to help me." And that builds relationships for life. It can be something as small as making a simple phone call. Putting people together can form a real permanent strategic alliance.

Know where you are so you can choose the appropriate action for the appropriate relationship. By seeing the results that a single connection can create in your life, in your business, and in your relationships, you will continue to create alliances.

Find a possible partnership between two businesses you have nothing to do with, but know there could be great synergy between them. Connect Company A with Company B.

A: ____

B: ____

Connect them today!

Make a difference and the money will follow

When I decided to go into business, I was not thinking about the money. I was thinking of fulfilling my passion by helping as many businesses as I could. I was thinking of creating a paradigm shift in the way that small businesses could access a marketing/public relations agency. I was thinking of making a difference.

Money followed, but it was not only about the money. I have met so many amazing people along this journey; I have seen places, shared experiences, and learned lessons. Those are rewards that money can't buy.

List three ways that you and your business can make a difference today:

1. ______________________________
2. ______________________________
3. ______________________________

Success is measured by how many people you help along the way. Start today!

Be a business owner, not self-employed

Being self-employed is shifting your paycheck from a company paying you to you paying yourself. When you shift your mentality and become a business owner, you become invested into your business. You are the driver of your success, and you can make it happen. The possibilities are endless. When you call yourself self-employed, you are limiting yourself. When you call yourself a business owner, you are taking the driver's seat of your success. It puts you at ease and helps you move to the next level, and that is the main difference between the two. A self-employed person will conform because they need to make the money. A business owner will do it because they are passionate about it, and they are ready to make a difference in the world.

Define your passion, put it into action, create value from nothing and then recognize that you are the driver of your success.

Shift your thinking from being self-employed to being a business owner, and write down what you observe. Ask yourself, "If I viewed myself as a business owner instead of being self-employed, what would I be doing differently?" List your answers:

____

____

____

____

____

____

Select the answer above that will have the greatest impact on your business, and do that one first.

Know the advantages of having a commercial office space

Working at home is great, and has many advantages. However, not having a commercial space can show a lack of stability to some prospects. Having a separate office will enable you to focus your attention and your actions on getting specific things done. As you create a place for yourself to work, it becomes habit for you to work there. Commercial office space will professionalize your business. You create stability in the eyes of your prospects. In commercial space, you can host your clients and power partners, as well as provide a site for seminars. You have more room to hire and expand your business.

If you don't have commercial office space, look at options for renting, buying, leasing, or sub-leasing office space that is more suitable to your business.

Do some research in the local area for affordable space.

Check with your accountant to ensure that you have the cash flow to make this happen.

File for the right type of business based on your situation

Many times, entrepreneurs do not know which business structure best suits them. It is important to define what type of business is best for you, whether sole proprietor, LLC, or corporation.

If you file for the right type of business, you can legally maximize your benefits of being in business. You need to seek guidance from your attorney and your accountant to make sure that you make the correct choice.

I started up as a sole proprietorship. After we purchased our first home and had more assets, and our office, I moved on to an LLC a couple of years later. That has worked out perfectly and gives us the protection we need.

Contact your attorney and accountant to find out how you can maximize your business type.

Set a date annually to assess your growth.

Take calculated risks

People say going into business is a risk. Guess what? Life is a risk. Taking a risk in business is living. There is a difference between risk without any foundation and calculated risks, however.

Follow your instincts, and follow the advice of others who have been there so that your risk is minimized. Tap into the resources of those who have been there, and use their knowledge. Utilize a conservative approach all around, as this minimizes the risk. Plan and lay out a foundation for your business, and develop an action plan to reach your goal.

Protect your business and your clients. Identify people you can trust by having them earn your trust. Maintain the confidentiality of your business and your clients, and everyone will win. Being conservative will help you minimize the risks.

Develop:

☐ *Non-disclosure agreement*

☐ *Non-compete agreement*

It's better to be safe than sorry.

Be cautious when having family as clients

The result of working with your family is frustrating sometimes. Although it is human nature to go to your family and closest friends when embarking on a new project, they can also be your worst critics. If you really want to work with family members, make sure that the rules and expectations are clearly specified so that your emotional ties don't confuse the objectives of your business relationships. In other words, because of the emotional connection, you have to be stricter than in a regular business relationship. If you do this, you will ensure a good client relationship, but also earn respect as the expert.

Create a list of five prospective clients who are not family members.

1. ______________________________
2. ______________________________
3. ______________________________
4. ______________________________
5. ______________________________

Be frugal

We give to others but sometimes we forget about ourselves. That can make or break your business. Being frugal does not mean being cheap. It means being alert and being conservative in the way you spend money. Take 10 percent off the top, and stick it in a rainy day bank account. Do not use it unless you absolutely need it. This puts you in the habit, even in the worst months, of putting 10 percent aside right off the top. Establish your budget for the year. You will be better prepared for an emergency and reduce your stress.

Create a savings plan this month!

Name three places in your business where you could cut expenses:

1. ______________________________
2. ______________________________
3. ______________________________

029

Control growth; don't let growth control you

Managed growth can grow a business; unmanaged growth can kill a business. The thought of growth is exciting, but if you don't have everything in place - the process, formula, steps, or logistics - to help you sustain that growth, the bad reputation can kill you. If you refuse to put in place all the logistics that you need to embrace the growth, it could be detrimental to your success. When you can't deliver your products, people complain. If you know that you have a big project coming up, ask for help. If you manage your growth, you can create a sustainable foundation to continue growing, and you will be a happy entrepreneur.

Create a formula for growth. Think of ways you can grow your business. Think of the steps that you need to take to embrace that growth.

Monitor your growth constantly to ensure you are growing.

030

Find what activity within your business excites you the most

What energizes you the most in your business? In my case, I love to connect with people by attending events, doing presentations, and simply communicating with clients. Doing what I love in my business allows me to enjoy my profession more, and it energizes me. My husband and partner, Juan Pablo, loves to work on creative designs, mostly behind the scenes, but we both do what we enjoy. The results are incredible as we synergize our strengths.

By doing what energizes you and leaving the things that you do not do well to others, you can be more proactive. You can create an environment of success and bliss.

Name at least one area in your business that excites you.

____

____

____

How will you use those strengths today to get you to the next level?

____

____

____

Define your talents and duplicate them

We all have different things we can give to the world both personally and professionally. We sometimes focus on our weaknesses, but if we can find our strengths and duplicate them, we become much stronger. If you have a particular strength, such as conveying messages by speaking, and if you can duplicate and strengthen that talent, it can move you to the next level. It can raise you from ordinary to extraordinary. Focus on the things you do well, and your talents will shine.

List your talents:

____

____

____

What can you do to reinforce them this week?

____

____

____

Keep your eye on your goal

We often embark on new goals but forget to check our progress and sometimes even forget the original goal. With so many distractions, it is easy to lose sight of our goals. For example, during my career as an entrepreneur, I have had a lot of great opportunities to work for other companies. I graciously turned them down because, although tempting, they have not been in line with my goal of being a successful entrepreneur. I constantly ask myself, "Is this situation getting me closer or further away from my goal?" If the answer is further away, then I simply don't engage in it. It's that easy!

There are three steps to this secret:

1. *Know your goal.*
2. *Remind yourself of your goal everyday, preferably with a written representation.*
3. *Constantly ask yourself: "Is this activity getting me closer or further away from my goal?"*

Apply the steps above to reach every one of your goals.

033

Create an exit strategy

You never know what is going to happen, so always have Plan B and Plan C in place. People think about starting a business, but they never think about how they are going to end that business. What would happen if you were no longer here? What would happen if you got sick or you moved? What is your exit strategy? Are you going to sell the business, dissolve the business, or merge with another company? Maybe you will have the business for the rest of your life, and your exit strategy will be retiring. Think ahead so you can feel prepared and ready to make the decisions you need to make.

What is your exit strategy?

☐ *Sell*
☐ *Retire*
☐ *Merge*
☐ *Dissolve*
☐ *Pass on to the next generation*

Plan ahead; it's worth it!

Seek clarity to make the right decisions

We make decisions constantly—decisions about who to hire, who to work with, how to spend our money, but are we making the right decisions?

It is only natural to want specific answers to our questions, but if we would only ask for clarity, it would be a much easier process. When I am faced with a decision, especially a difficult one, I ask diligently for clarity by using affirmations like the one below.

Constantly seek guidance for your life, and you will be successful. All the answers to your questions are inside you. Program clarity into your heart and mind in a way that communicates it clearly and effectively so that you can act on it when the right decision is revealed to you.

Fill in the blank below:
"I am grateful now that I have clarity and confidence to make the decision to________________________________."

Three times a day for the next month, repeat this affirmation until it takes root and moves you forward.

Say it with the belief that it is going to work!

Visit **www.bizsecretsthatwork.com/affirmations.pdf** to download a free form to create your own affirmations.

Get support

We may have negative people around us and, unfortunately, those people may be our family and friends. You receive your motivation and excitement from your surroundings, so make a conscious decision to surround yourself with people who have similar goals and objectives as yours. Identify people who are positive and who make you feel good when you speak with them. If you are down, they will lift you up. Find people who will share with you their knowledge about a subject and share resources with you if needed. Find people who are smarter than you, people who are more positive, so when you are going through a difficult time in your life, you can count on those people to help you get out of that negative circle and get away from the people who are dragging you down. Stay away from the people who are creating a negative impact in your life. You will be much more energized and motivated. Most importantly, you will have a core system when you need it.

Identify three positive people in your life:

1. ______________________________

2. ______________________________

3. ______________________________

For the next week set up an appointment to meet with them.

Section 2
Sales

Sales is a process, and we can all learn something in this area. We are constantly selling ourselves, whether we recognize it or not. These simple secrets will give you the know-how to maximize this numbers' game.

Keep your antenna up

The prospect that you least expect might turn out to be your biggest client. One of my mentors shared an interesting anecdote of how she started working with a small cleaning products company that barely had any money. She knew that they had a small budget, but she felt the need to help them. Surprisingly, this company grew a great deal after landing a contract with a big box retailer. Just a few years later, the company was a multimillion-dollar enterprise and she grew with them, too. Being open to new client opportunities can be the difference between landing that big client or not. Remember that a seemingly small prospect could turn into a big client if you believe in them. Stay alert.

List five of your prospects here:

____

____

____

____

____

What hidden potential do you see in each?

Be brave enough to approach them with your ideas to take them to the next level without giving them everything.

Align yourself with power partners

There is no such thing as competition. The competitors might as well be called "power partners." Instead of competing, the technique that I have always used is to create allies in business. My approach has turned what were negative situations into situations of collaboration. I work with other marketing agencies and distributors to utilize their core competencies for the benefit of my clients. On one occasion, I was working with a client who needed more exposure in the marketplace. We created a multi-channel marketing strategy that integrated various channels of communications. I decided to partner with a social media expert to get the most viral marketing effect for the campaign. I completed the overall strategy, and the company focused on the social network expertise. The end result was success for everyone involved. To clients, alliances between two companies bring the best of both for their benefit. Find some power partners, bring them to your clients, and be a hero.

Can you identify an ally?
☐ Yes ☐ No

What unique selling propositions do they bring to the table that you don't have?

____
____
____

I will contact the following companies to define some ways to collaborate:

A ______________________________________
B ______________________________________
C ______________________________________

038

Let your success stories be your sales team

When you are dealing with a new client and have limited time to go into every experience with previous clients, it's nice to have testimonials to showcase your talents. Testimonials might be in writing, on video, or even in audio files for your prospects to experience. This might be the difference between landing the job and walking away without it.

What clients have you benefitted lately? Will you ask them to write a testimonial?

I plan to use those testimonials in the following ways to gain more business:

____

____

____

____

____

Testimonials are a wonderful way to get more clients. Use them strategically!

Know your conversion ratio

Sales is a numbers game, and knowing your industry's and your company's conversion ratios are critical. What is the contact-to-appointment ratio and the appointment-to-sales ratio for your company? Take the next three weeks to figure this out.

Set goals on how many people you will contact and define your goals for these appointments. In addition, how many sales will you close from those appointments? Do this exercise for at least three consecutive weeks, and you will begin to figure out what those ratios are. Knowing this will be extremely important because your expectations will be set.

Fill in the numbers that reflect your goals.

_______calls = _______appointments

_______appointments = ________sales (closed clients)

Use these results to create your sales strategy.

Have flexibility to work with different types of clients

Diversity is all around us. Customer relations are not the exception. At times, you may find a customer who is really hands-on, but at other times, you might work with a customer who is completely laid back. As you begin any relationship, seek cues as to their style so that you can maximize your relationship.

For example, if you are working with hands-on customers, try to get them involved, constantly communicate with them and look for feedback. On the other hand, with a laid back customer, provide sporadic progress updates that are easy to read and understand without providing many details. Having the flexibility to work with different types of customers will give you a competitive advantage over other companies and allow you to be open to new possibilities.

What can I do this week to adjust to my current customers?

Customer A: ______________________________

____

Customer B: ______________________________

____

Customer C: ______________________________

____

Send thank you cards

A simple hand-written thank you note goes a long way. As an employee or "intrapreneur" (an entrepreneur inside another company), I wrote more than 4,000 thank you cards in three years. Every Friday, I took time to write thank you cards to all the people that I met that week.

This gesture allowed me to create an emotional connection with most of the people I came into contact with and created a very good impression, as well. Writing thank you cards has been one of the most powerful activities in my career for creating good relationships. You, too, can use this tactic to build great relationships!

Write down people to whom you will send a thank you card this week:

____

____

____

____

____

SendOutCards.com has been an incredible tool for me.
I encourage you to try it.

Build the list

It has never been so important to build a contact list. I have been building mine for the last several years, diligently connecting with incredible people along the way. This list has paid off for my business and has been a leveraging tool for great opportunities.

I started building my list when I was 18 years old. Nobody told me to keep a list or to communicate with the people on it. I simply knew that this would someday be beneficial in my career. I attended several events, joined several organizations, and gave presentations. It is never too late to start your own list. You can build it by attending networking events, seeking referrals, adding a sign-in box on your website and e-mails, doing cross-promotions with other businesses, etc.

Write down the two activities that you will do this week to start/build your own list:

1. ____

2. ____

It's never too late to start building your list!

Show what you can do

We live in the "now" generation. Everybody wants things now. One thing that we have experienced with generation Y and generation X is that we have a sense of entitlement in business: a "me" attitude. The problem is that you have to be willing to give before you receive. This sense of "you have to give me a raise because I am me, you have to give me this business because I am me, you have to give me this much because I am me," does not work to create relationships. That is the problem. It is important to know that by giving first, by being willing to show what you can do, and the value you can bring to that relationship, you can really make a difference in your career.

One thing I did with a previous employer was to create a marketing department. For a long time, I went above and beyond without asking for a raise. I was bringing in money and new clients. One day (and no one told me this, I just had it somewhere in my mind, probably from my early days with Zig Ziglar and Dale Carnegie's readings), I knew that in order to request a raise, I had to go in and show them my value. So, I spent a weekend writing down all the things that I did. I documented all the value that I brought to the organization, as well as the things that I was willing to do to continue to bring value. I wrote down about 30 bullet points on nice letterhead with an introduction paragraph. I sat down with the two owners, handed the letter to them, and asked, "Can you please give me five minutes of your time?" They did not have a lot of time, so I just focused on the bullet points. They were impressed because they were not aware of all the value I brought to the organization. I looked them straight in the eye and said, "I need a $10,000 raise." On the spot, they gave me a $6,500 raise. About two months later, they gave me another $3,500 raise plus started giving me commission, too. Within a few months of my initial request (based on the way I positioned myself, showed value before I was expecting to receive anything, and the commitment that I was willing to put into this) they gave me an $11,000 raise!

When I tell this story, people are shocked, because no one gives you an $11,000 raise. But, how you present yourself is what matters. So, if you go above and beyond, and if you give before you receive, you can build a genuine relationship and get anything you want in the end. Anything you wish for (and more) will be there.

List some requirements of your job or a particular client project:

____

____

____

Select one added responsibility you can contribute over the next few weeks and report on that activity constantly to your superior.

____

____

____

Work on exceeding these requirements for the next six months.

Everything else will come.

Really, really listen

We think about ourselves and what we want. But the first meeting with a client should be about listening to them. They do not care about you; they care about how you are going to make an impact on their business. Make the conversation all about them. You have two ears and one mouth, so you can listen twice as much as you talk. You'll find your customer's needs and wants by listening. You will connect with your customer and can provide the service that the customer is looking for, and that will lead to a happy ending for both the customer and you. You also will build a relationship for life.

In all meetings you have this week, listen. Make it all about the person you are meeting with.

Name three ways you can become a better listener this week:

1. ____
2. ____
3. ____

045

Show you care...

"People don't care how much you know, but how much you care," Tom Gosche, *The Business Strategist* enthusiastically said to me during a conversation.

Tom elaborated by saying that if you are not adding value for your customer by offering more than just the product and service, you are not doing a good job. Don't worry so much about the presentation and the product–worry about making a connection with your prospect. For example, listen twice as much as you talk during the presentation, paraphrase your prospect's comments to ensure understanding and reflect back to a comment they made during the meeting to show them you listened.

People want to do business with people they trust. Showing your customers you care can lead to repeat business and can build relationships. In essence, the more you give, the more you get back in return.

What will you do this week to show you care?

___

___

___

___

Have an end result in mind for every client

Many times, we engage in relationships with clients seeking our reward, but you should focus on your client's reward instead. Visualize how your services will make an impact on that client. The end result for all of your clients should be their success. By being focused on that, you are able to create actions which can lead to a lasting relationship. You are there to create success for them. Even if success is not immediate, if clients feel that you are there to support them every step of the way, they will realize that all your energy is going into making them successful.

Ask clients what they want as an end result of your relationship. By doing so, you build a good reputation, you create an emotional connection, and you foster loyalty.

What is the end result when you engage with a new customer?

____

____

____

____

Have that end result present in your mind every step of the way.

Constantly feed the sales funnel

You always have ups and downs; that is the nature of business. There will always be a roller coaster effect. To minimize that, you must feed the sales funnel constantly. How many phone calls are you going to make this week? How many presentations will you give? What is the phone call-to-appointment ratio? Define a sales plan or strategy for the next three to six months. Find out what you need to do to minimize the roller coaster effect as a business professional.

Determine the top three activities you must do constantly to feed the funnel:

____

____

____

Visit **www.bizsecretsthatwork.com/funnel.pdf**
to download a free sales/marketing funnel template.

048

Get serious about service

All businesses say they have great customer service, but customer service is not a static event; it is an ongoing process. It constantly moves and challenges you. Every project you do, is always a test of your service. Being service-oriented is not about doing one thing one day. It is about being there constantly, making it a habit to service your clients.

Service is what differentiates you from other businesses and helps you create an emotional connection. You want to make your customers feel you are going above and beyond to serve them. You will build more relationships and new clients this way.

Write down ways in which you can enhance your customer service:

____

____

____

____

____

____

List them and take the action.

049

Be firm and confident about rates and deliverables

See the value of charging for your services. Oftentimes, we bend to accommodate the needs of others without compromise. If you change your fees without compromise, the client is going to see it as a weakness, and they might think your service is not worth what you were charging in the first place. If you are going to fluctuate your rates, the client has to be willing to compromise, as well. Be willing to say no and walk away from a deal. Being able to do so is very empowering. It lets people know you are not going to be a doormat. Standing firm on your price is essential because no one has the right to take advantage of you. Nothing will kill your business faster than being wishy-washy on your price.

Be willing to negotiate. Whenever you give something away, you have to take something away. If you are going to lower your price, you need to take something of value away to be fair.

Be firm on the price.

Stop guessing

Guessing what your customers want and how to solve their problems will not get you anywhere. We live in a world that has gotten smaller due to technology. Whether your client is across the street or around the globe, the communication shift in the paradigm during the last few years has made it easy for us to reach out and obtain information almost instantly. Whatever your question or problem is, there are solutions and resources. Take advantage of technology and ask questions. Do research. Stop guessing. Inquiring information might be the difference between getting that big client and not.

Stop guessing this week.

Do one of the following:

- ☐ *Pick up the phone to interview your customers.*
- ☐ *Do research on a topic with which you are not familiar.*
- ☐ *Find statistics from legitimate and reputable sources.*

051

Find customers with multiple departments and big budgets

When you have small companies as clients, you need to have many of them. But when you align with a larger company, it gives you the opportunity to work on larger projects. Do your research, and find out as much information as you can about a prospect. There is greater stability in a larger company, making your company more stable and giving your company more credibility. This helps you grow and diversify your business.

Recognize that the sales cycle for bigger companies is much longer and more complicated than for a smaller company.

Identify one well-known business or one company that you can go after.

Company I will target this year:

____

Make sure you can service them, and don't be intimidated!

Be specific on proposals

If you are not specific on proposals, people don't get a sense of customization. They feel that they are just another number.

If you present factual and objective information about the company that you are sending the proposal to, clients will be impressed to know that you took the time to listen to them. Small businesses have the ability to truly connect with prospects since most of the time, it is the business owner that is presenting the proposal. Proposals are a great way to prove that you understand your prospect's needs. Use this tool wisely!

Look at your current proposals.

What feature or features can you add to your proposals to make them more personalized for each client?

____

____

____

____

Prioritize

This is the epitome of keeping control of our lives. We think everything is urgent and everything is important, but it is not. There are certain things that have to be done today, but the rest of the items are not urgent. You want to be in control of everything, but you have to learn that you can't be. Instead, you have to prioritize. By prioritizing, you can find time to do the things that are important.

Create a list of action items, and highlight the three top priorities.

____

____

____

____

____

____

____

Focus on those priorities today, and don't be distracted by the other items on your list.

Focus on sustainable growth

If something sounds too easy, it is probably not a wise way to grow your business. Sustainable growth is based on a foundation of ethical behavior and on being authentic and true to yourself. Focus on activities that move you closer to your objectives. Usually when something grows too fast, it also has the potential to collapse as fast.

What is it that you envision for your growth?

____

____

____

What steps can you take this week to make that growth sustainable?

____

____

____

____

____

Create an emotional connection

When you focus on creating and building relationships, you create an emotional connection. This is my credo; it is the way I live my life. I create relationships with people I come into contact with: employees, clients and vendors. One of the most important ways to create an emotional connection is by listening to them and by being totally present for that person. Do not just hear, but *listen,* and you will build relationships for life.

The phrase "emotional connection" has become a part of my everyday life. If a client has a particular like, such as dogs, you can mention that in dealing with them or give them a small gift for their dog.

Creating an emotional connection is all about thinking of the other person and giving before you ever receive. The core of life is about building an emotional connection with the people you deal with professionally or personally.

This week, do something special for one person based on his or her personal interest.

*Who?*____

*What will I do?*________________________________

____

You can learn more about what this person likes by simply asking.

Promote your business through third-party endorsements

Every business needs exposure and awareness. We rely on ourselves to do everything, but you don't have to. You can actually create an affect where people refer your business on an ongoing basis. Inevitably, other businesses will begin spreading the word if you deliver results for your clients. That is why it is so important to focus on the success of your clients.

When somebody else is talking about you , it is 10 times more powerful than when you are talking about yourself. If you deliver, you will have people speaking highly of you and bringing you more business.

For the next week:

What traits do I want my clients to tell others about?

___

___

___

Big fish, small fish, you decide

Same type of work. Half the price. You decide!

It is curious how a small client paying a fraction of the cost will demand more of your time and energy. Let's face it, we are in business to make money, and it is OK to work with small clients. But be cautious and do not let the relationship enter a vicious cycle of unnecessary demands.

List your three most demanding small clients

$ # of Hours

Client 1 ____

Client 2 ____

Client 3 ____

How much are you making with these three clients?

$__________ / __________hours worked = ________hourly rate

Now do the same for three less demanding, larger clients

$ # of Hours

Client 1 ____

Client 2 ____

Client 3 ____

How much are you making with these three clients?

$__________ / __________hours worked = ________hourly rate

You do the math!

Working with profitable clients not only frees up some of your time, but you will also feel more energized!

Section 3
Marketing

Marketing is a fascinating tool that can be the difference between survival and failure. In this ever-changing world, the choice of marketing tools available is endless. There are no limits on how you can market your business. These secrets will provide you with the marketing tips that you need to succeed.

Identify your audience

The single most important aspect of marketing is to define your target audience. A lot of businesses waste money marketing to the wrong audiences. As an owner of a marketing agency, I help clients target the right audience all the time. Defining a target audience means taking into consideration demographics (i.e., gender and age), geographics (i.e., physical location), and psychographics (i.e., lifestyle). The more information you can obtain, the more you will maximize your marketing dollars.

Taking five of your current clients, define the following elements:

	Age	Gender	Race	Income	Education
1					
2					
3					
4					
5					

Looking at the five clients above, you should begin to notice some patterns. Out of these clients, think about the ones you enjoy working with most. As you market your business, take the focused approach, not the "spray and pray" approach. The results will speak for themselves.

Take a bird's eye view of your brand

Have you asked your customers what they want? Have you asked them how they perceive your company and what impact it has on their business? This allows you to objectively look at your business and your brand. Your brand is the most important asset you have. For example, when you think of Apple, you think of quality, freshness, and technology just by seeing the brand. When you think of McDonald's, you think about fast food, affordability, and consistency. You must get into the hearts and minds of your clients. How does your brand make them feel?

Form a focus group to identify how your brand makes people feel. Ask your customers directly how they feel!

Based on the results, consider re-branding or making adjustments as necessary.

Create key messages

A very important step once you have defined your target audience is to define what messages resonate with them. Talk about their interests, likes, and special events. Birthday and anniversary programs have an extremely high success rate because you are talking to your clients about events that are important to them. You are connecting with your audience emotionally by taking the time to acknowledge what it is that matters the most to them. Two things to consider in creating key messages for your target audience are a) timing and b) relevance.

Remember, you don't have to be everything to everyone. It is OK to be clear about who your ideal target audience is.

Communicate in their language when talking to them and remember: timing and relevance.

Survey three clients with these questions.

Client 1: ____

Client 2: ____

Client 3: ____

- How did you hear about us?
- Why did you choose us?
- What is most important about our relationship (value and benefits)?
- When is your birthday and anniversary?

Use the right vehicles

Marketing can make or break a company. Defining the target audience and key messages is as important as defining the right vehicles to reach your clients. For example, a product for seniors is not likely to gain a lot of exposure in marketing via social media vehicles. The senior community is simply not going to feel as comfortable using new marketing trends as they are with traditional marketing vehicles such as direct mail and catalog buying. Using the right vehicles to reach your audience can save you time and money.

Define three marketing vehicles that you can use to effectively reach your audience:

Vehicle 1: ______________________________
Vehicle 2: ______________________________
Vehicle 3: ______________________________

Sample list:

- *Testimonials as third party endorsements*
- *Cross (introduce other products) and up selling (upgrades to existing products)*
- *Position yourself as an expert*
- *List your business free on online portals*
- *Host an open house event*
- *Build a strong database*
- *Create a news release with a unique angle*
- *Book a speaking engagement*
- *Advertise in a local paper*
- *Create a newsletter or e-blast*

Create a marketing plan

Marketing is crucial to the success of any company. It is the one thing that you can create, change, or control to impact the bottom line. A good marketing plan should include the following elements:

1. About the Company
2. Brand Identifiers
3. SWOT Analysis
4. Strategy and Tactics
5. Marketing Funnel
6. Marketing Calendar

A marketing plan is the roadmap that propels your success. It is often used as a portion of a business plan and aids in getting loans or grants. Ultimately, investors want to know how you plan on creating revenue, and a good marketing plan will help prove that.

Create or revise your marketing plan this month.

What of the six elements could you beef up to improve your marketing plan?

Having a marketing plan will drive your business to success!

Develop a marketing calendar

A marketing plan should include a marketing calendar, which is the physical visualization of the marketing strategy. Many businesses have a marketing plan, but they might not implement it because they simply don't understand it. Having a marketing calendar or visual timeline allows businesses to understand their plan to the fullest and therefore execute it properly and in a timely manner. A marketing calendar can contain the tactics for the next three years, one year, or simply the timeline for a single project.

Create a marketing calendar today.

Visit **www.bizsecretsthatwork.com/mktcalendar.pdf** to access a free marketing calendar template.

Market more, not less

In business, when things turn bad financially, the first thing that often gets cut is marketing. Companies do not realize marketing is so important, especially during difficult financial times. According to a survey by McGraw & Hill conducted after the 1981-1982 recession, companies that continued their marketing gained an average of 256 percent in market share by 1985, as well as gaining incredible customer loyalty.

There are many cost-effective ways to market your business. The world is your market. Deploy techniques that allow you to reach more of your target market with a limited budget.

List things you can do this week to market your business.

____

____

____

____

____

____

____

____

____

____

____

Consider creating a newsletter, attending an event, creating a social media account, learning about text messaging, or updating your website.

Know the benefits of regular communications

Hard copy communications, such as bulletins or newsletters mailed to customers or prospects, e-mails, postings in social media, or whatever the vehicle might be to regularly communicate with your clients is so important. You must stay in contact with them to generate business, incremental revenue, an emotional connection, credibility, and loyalty. Simply stay in touch regularly with the people with whom you do business. This gives your company a sense of stability.

What type of regular communication will you launch this week? It can be a newsletter or bulletin, social media updates, or text messaging. Assign a schedule for this communication and stick to it.

Sign up to receive our monthly newsletter at
www.jjrmarketing.com

066

Stay abreast of current trends in the marketplace

We can become stagnant in the marketplace, but the way that we do business continues to evolve. Embrace new marketing trends, such as social media, to drive more people to your website and generate more business. Realize what is shifting in the marketplace. Know what's going on, conduct research, and read articles. What is happening in your industry? How can you take advantage of those changes that are happening right now?

This week, spend some time conducting research and reading articles to keep abreast of trends.

Maximize opportunities and gain business.

Create an excellent business reputation

Every morning, I read the "Optimist Creed" by Christian D. Larson. "I promise myself to be so strong that nothing can disturb my peace of mind. To talk happiness and prosperity to every person I meet. To make all my friends feel that there's something worthwhile in them. To look at the sunny side of everything and make my optimism come true. To think only of the best, to work only for the best, and to expect only the best. To be just as enthusiastic about the success of others as I am about my own. To forget the mistakes of the past and press on to the great achievements of the future. To wear a cheerful expression at all times and give a smile to every living creature I meet. To give so much to improving myself that I have no time to criticize others. To be too large for worry, too noble for anger, too strong for fear and too happy to permit the presence of trouble. To think well of myself and proclaim this fact to the world, not in loud words but in great deeds. To live in the faith that the whole world is on my side as long as I am true to the best values in me."

My father had a saying: "Create a good reputation and fall asleep." I agree partially with this statement. I don't want to have a good reputation and then sleep. I want to create a good reputation and continue building a great reputation. You have a responsibility to ensure you continue that excellence in your reputation. Always do the right thing, and always follow your heart. The foundation of any good, sustainable business is integrity. When you create an excellent reputation, everything else comes to you: business opportunities, money, and whatever else you desire. You create reasons for people to contact you and give you business. The "Optimist Creed" reminds me of that every morning.

You create an excellent reputation by expecting it of yourself and living it yourself. Then take your reputation and share it with your clients, your business associates, your colleagues, or even your family.

Choose one of the following for this week:

☐ *Define three of your core values.*

☐ *Give your word, and keep your word.*

☐ *Tell your clients you'll have it done in seven days, and get it done in two.*

An excellent reputation is built by one person, one moment at a time. You're not only delivering on it for them; you're also delivering on it for yourself.

Position yourself as an expert

You can't be everything to everyone, so defining your niche is imperative. If you are a catering company, you can define a special segment of expertise, such as "the best caterer for corporate events," and market yourself that way. This doesn't mean you don't cater other types of events. It simply positions you as an expert in an area; ideally the one that is most profitable for you. Positioning yourself as an expert not only opens new doors of opportunity, but it also can provide you with public relations exposure.

What are you best at?

What step will you take today to let the marketplace know that?

Seek speaking engagements

How else can you get in front of multiple possible prospects? By speaking, you are able to share your expertise, create exposure, and most importantly, generate interest in your company in front of a captive audience. Many local organizations are seeking to have experts engage their groups.

Create a list of some topics you feel comfortable speaking about:

____

____

____

____

____

____

What organizations can you contact this month to get the ball rolling?

____

____

____

____

____

____

Maximize resources

People do not use their resources (memberships, allocated funds, etc.) wisely. Maximizing your resources could be the difference between losing time and money and growing success. You must determine how you are using your resources and maximize them to the best of your ability so that you are getting your money's worth. Encourage yourself to take full advantage of your resources.

Make a list of items you have that you are not using to the maximum.

____

____

____

____

What will you do today to maximize those resources?

____

____

____

____

Find out about local awards

Every business needs visibility and there are always award opportunities in your local area. Whether the award is small or large, the recognition that goes with it is invaluable. You can nominate your company for an award. By simply being a nominee, the marketing and public relations opportunities can be incredible. Take, for example, my experience as a multi-award winner. I was a nominee and then one of two finalists as Latina Entrepreneur of the Year. Although I did not take the latter award home, all the exposure before, during, and after the gala was second to none. I had a camera crew come to my office for the ceremony video (similar to the Oscars, but on a smaller scale, of course), and information was posted on the organization's website, and sent out to more than 45,000 e-mail subscribers. The value of the exposure was incredible. I saw an immediate increase in business.

Research two or three award opportunities in your area this week.

Nominate your company!

It's all about marketing

There are a lot of marketing opportunities for your business, but sometimes those opportunities go unnoticed. Consider the following: attending a networking event with a strong follow-up campaign, posting new information about your company on your website, participating in social networks, creating an e-mail signature, distributing a newsletter, advertising in local newspapers, online directories, etc. If you are the keynote speaker at an event, consider marketing the event before in your newsletter, local publications, and on your website. During the presentation, sell and distribute your book, white paper, or membership, and collect information about the attendees. After the event, conduct a strong follow-up campaign, and add the attendees to your database and client relationship management (CRM) program/software for future communications across multiple vehicles.

Every aspect of your business has the opportunity to be exposed across multiple marketing vehicles and touchpoints. Knowing that it takes five to seven times for people to remember your brand, it is a great idea to maximize every opportunity you have. Think outside the box when thinking marketing. Think of EVERY way that you market your product, service, or event for maximum results!

Define one aspect of your business you can promote this month:

List methods and vehicles to market it:

See how you can maximize your exposure cost-effectively!

Make a difference in the marketplace

To create a business that orchestrates a shift in the paradigm, you must continue to adapt to new circumstances in the market. Based on feedback from your customers, visualize what the world would be like if your company wasn't there. What difference are you making in their lives? The uniqueness you bring to the table makes a difference. Be an individual, and think about the impact you're making by engaging with their company. Would the customer have succeeded if you weren't around? Think about the impact you are making in the marketplace and the reputation that you have in your industry. When you make decisions based on your heart and based on making a true difference in the world and in the marketplace, you become a magnet that other people seek out.

Think of one client and how you have impacted their business. What would life be like for them without you?

____

____

____

____

____

Capture your ideas in writing

Writing down your ideas solidifies them, puts them in perspective, and gets them ready for evaluation and execution. We all have many ideas, but many times, they disappear just like smoke in the air. A few years ago, I decided I would consciously capture all of my ideas, similar to a brainstorming session without being judgmental. I decided that I would take those ideas, write them down, analyze them and make them happen. There is something magical about writing things down; it helps you get closer to your goals.

Write down three ideas for evaluation:

*1*____

*2*____

*3*____

Rate the brilliance of each idea here (10 as the highest score):
Idea 1: ________
Idea 2: ________
Idea 3: ________

Make them happen!

075

Share good opportunities with others

You have been invited to an event that represents a great opportunity to meet potential customers. You have been given five exclusive tickets to the event but decide that giving them to anyone might detract from your potential exposure there. What do you do? Do you give them out to business colleagues or do you keep them to yourself? The truth is there are plenty of opportunities to go around for everyone. It is okay to share good opportunities with others. It means you will get more opportunities in return. Get ready for the event, and rent a limo for your colleagues as well!

Is there one good event that you can share with a colleague this month?

Event: ____

Who will I invite as my VIP guest? ______________________

Define the ingredients of a successful event

In my years of doing events for clients, I have found many times that people have one ingredient and miss out on other ones. They do not maximize all the opportunities that a good event can bring them. If you do not define the ingredients to a successful event, you lose out on a great opportunity for exposure and brand awareness. This is your chance to shine in front of prospects, vendors, clients, and media. By hosting events, ribbon-cutting ceremonies, and grand openings, you create a spotlight for yourself. Every component must create an impact. A number of things go into hosting an event. You definitely need to host at a convenient venue, and furnish food and drinks, entertainment, a presentation, a photographer to capture key moments, raffles, giveaways, networking opportunities, sponsorship opportunities, impeccable service, and a philanthropic partnership, which usually leads to being featured in the media.

These events reinforce your brand, create credibility, build trust, create third-party endorsements, and highlight opportunities to showcase your success. You connect with people emotionally and strengthen relationships.

Entertainment creates an environment. When people go to events, they go to connect. All these components work together like a well-oiled machine. These are important components for a successful event.

You acquire benefits from hosting an event. You will get credibility, connect with the audience, gain third-party endorsements, showcase your success, be featured in media outlets, and reinforce relationships and business opportunities.

What is the next event that you will host?

____

Date: ____________

Ingredients to a successful event (not in a specific order):

- ☐ *Convenient venue/location*
- ☐ *Food and drinks*
- ☐ *Entertainment*
- ☐ *Presentation*
- ☐ *Photographer*
- ☐ *Giveaways*
- ☐ *Raffle prizes*
- ☐ *Media*
- ☐ *Networking opportunities*
- ☐ *Sponsors*
- ☐ *Impeccable service*

Begin planning to ensure that you have all the components for success!

Launch a newsletter (or e-newsletter)

A newsletter is important because not only does it create loyalty, but it also positions you as an expert. It creates a constant communication device to stay in touch, and it gives you business opportunities. More than three years ago, I launched my "Make It Happen" newsletter. It was one of the early lessons I learned in life that was engraved in my brain.

With a newsletter (online or offline), you have a reason to stay in constant touch with your friends, clients, colleagues, vendors, and strategic alliances. It is a wonderful tool. From the get-go, I started featuring one local business, giving them some exposure. That newsletter has now become the epitome of a lot of my success. It is going strong and has given me more opportunity than I could have imagined generating incremental revenue and becoming a platform for the local business community (and even national community) to expose their knowledge and highlight them as experts.

I feature all kinds of local events, and people come to me and say, "Jackie, I am here because I saw it in your newsletter." People expect to receive my newsletter and often forward it on to someone else. It is an incredible opportunity for me to see that people are finding value in this newsletter. It is something that can start off like a little baby, and then grow. Be consistent. Send your newsletter around the same time each month so people begin to get excited about its arrival.

Newsletters are meant to build loyalty. The content must be 85 percent educational and 15 percent promotional. It takes time, but it is time well invested. Define the components that your audience wants to hear about in your newsletter and begin sending it. No questions asked, just do it. You will begin to see the magical relationships you build with it.

Decide on a schedule (monthly, quarterly, or semi-annually) and then stick to it. The amazing things that will come to you because of that will be immeasurable. You can build relationships, become an expert, and get exposure that you would not have thought about. Now, I have more than 5,000 people receiving my newsletter, and it is becoming bigger and bigger. The opportunities are endless.

Define the elements of your newsletter:

____

____

____

____

I am sending my first newsletter on:

____

How often will I send it?
Every ___________________________

Make sure that the content is valuable and resonates with the audience!

Keep your business goals present every day

Because we are so busy in our lives, we forget to stay on track of our goals, especially our business goals. Whether it is to close a certain number of sales, to do some marketing, or to make sure you stay within operating expenses, it is important to remind yourself of your business goals and keep them present in your life. This will help keep you focused and motivated to continue to achieve them. It is a process, a progressive series of steps that move you closer to the success you want in business.

Whether it is notes or your mission statement, look at it every day to remind yourself why you are doing what you do. For instance, my company's three core values are integrity, professionalism, and accountability, so I have those goals present every day. By reminding yourself of your goals, all of a sudden you will wake up one day and say, "Wow, look at all the things that I've achieved." Because I have never given up, I have never lost sight of my focus, and here I am. And that is the magical part about it. I think for me, as an entrepreneur, this simple act is one of the most important ingredients to my success. By having those goals present every day, not every week or every month, I am able to get closer to them faster than I could imagine.

Write down your goals and print them out. Place them in your office where you will have to look at them every day.

Know the benefits of direct mail

Direct mail is one of the oldest ways of marketing. Many people think that direct mail is going away because of the migration to online initiatives, but the truth is that it will never go away. Despite the shifts we've experienced with new marketing trends, this tool is still an important part of most businesses' marketing efforts. It is definitely experiencing some changes, and it will become more "interactive" and integrated with other marketing vehicles. For example, consider a doctor who is moving her practice. She utilizes direct mail to announce the move to her 6,000 patients with an oversized postcard embedded with an intelligent mail barcode (IMB). This code allows her to know when the drop date will be. She launches a recorded voice messaging campaign on Monday, letting her patients know that they will receive the "move notification" on Wednesday. She directs patients to the website for more information. The integration of multiple touchpoints across vehicles allows her to maximize the announcement, and the campaign is a huge success!

Direct mail has many faces and can be integrated with many other vehicles.

- *Direct mail with variable data: features the name of the recipient on multiple locations of the mailing piece, i.e., John, with a third-party incentive and call of action.*
- *Direct mail with IBC: embeds a tracking code that provides a two-day delivery date window, combined with voice messaging campaign.*
- *Direct mail with PURLs: variable data with a personalized URL, i.e., John.Smith.yourcampaignname.com. About 42 percent of the people who receive a mailing piece prefer to respond online.*

Create a campaign using direct mail this quarter. Make sure that you combine the campaign with at least one other vehicle.

Experiential marketing

You can resonate with your audience by creating experiences through marketing. At Starbucks, for example, people come in to buy a $4 cup of coffee not because the coffee is better than at McDonald's but because of the surroundings. People are buying an experience and the feelings that it evokes. Going out to dinner at a fine restaurant is not usually for the food but for the experience, the music, and the ambience.

You can create that with marketing when you send out a postcard. Go beyond the message. What type of experience do readers get with the imagery you use? You can use this for every customer touchpoint.

Experiential marketing can create an emotional connection with people because you are going beyond the basics and giving them what they cannot get anywhere else.

Test experiential marketing for yourself. Go to one of your favorite places and be aware of your surroundings: the music, and how the experience of being there makes you feel.

Write your findings here:

____

____

____

How can you use these findings to make a difference in your business?

____

____

____

Market with articles or white papers

If you have a lot of experience on a certain topic and don't have the time or the resources to write a complete book, you might consider creating articles or white papers. These tools are fairly easy to create and can position you as an expert. The key to these is to have a "soft sale" approach and focus on the benefits to the reader instead of the features of your company.

Once created, you can use them in several ways:

- *Post on your website as a call-to-action for visitors*
- *Distribute at events and speaking engagements*
- *Send to existing clients*
- *Post on social networks*
- *Send to local newspapers or magazine editors*
- *Upload to online portals (directories)*
- *Send to strategic partners for possible inclusion in their newsletters or on their websites*

Create one article this week and use some of the distribution ideas listed above.

As you can see, marketing your article is easier than you think!

Use social media to your advantage

Social media has created a shift in the way we communicate. Whether we like it or not, social media is here to stay, and you can incorporate it in your marketing mix. It is an affordable medium that allows you to reach the masses via a viral marketing effect. Consider this: I have about 221 people in my immediate network on LinkedIn. Each of my connections might also have a network similar to mine or bigger. And their connections might have the same, and so on. Imagine the number of people that I can reach. Because social media is 100 percent permission-based, it allows me to be in touch with the people I trust and who trust me. Take advantage of this incredible opportunity to market your business!

Do you have an account on the following?:

☐ *LinkedIn*
☐ *Facebook*
☐ *Twitter*
☐ *Plaxo*

If you don't, create them this week.

Once you've created these accounts, use this free tool to make simultaneous posts on all of your accounts: www.ping.fm.

Create reciprocal links online

Because the way the world communicates is shifting, it is extremely important to recognize that just a website does not get you anywhere anymore. The bar is being set higher and higher. The same way you network in person applies to networking online. When people connect you with somebody and then you connect with somebody else, you get noticed. As we become more competitive, we must be noticed online. One of the ways we get noticed online is by creating reciprocal links. The more links you have pointing to and from your website, the more the search engines will recognize your website. Then, you will get pulled up when people type those keywords into search engines. An easy way to create reciprocal links going back to your website is to create co-op opportunities with your clients. They are completely free. It is a matter of going that extra mile and saying, "Hey, I would love to put a link to your website on one of our web pages." You create a win-win situation for both parties, and you both get exposure. The more links you have going to and from your website, the more noticed you will be online, and the easier it will be for people to find you. This is easy and cost-effective and can really increase leads.

Research some portals, both horizontal and vertical, where you can list your company for free. Contact local businesses and ask to reciprocate links, too.

Use public relations wisely

Public relations can have a very positive impact on any company, if used correctly. Messages in a public relations campaign should be focused on a unique angle that attracts public attention, not used as a self-serving tool. Messages should be important and educate the target audience of that specific publication or electronic media. Businesses can also notify their local media about anniversaries, special events, new products, partnerships with not-for-profit organizations, etc. It is not guaranteed that the event will be featured, but don't give up.

An effective public relations campaign should include the following steps:

- *Distributing news releases to media outlets*
- *Following up with media*
- *Setting up interviews with media (when interested)*
- *Collecting clippings*
- *Sharing the editorial features with clients, posting them on your website, sending them to strategic partners and prospects, etc.*

No matter how great you are, nothing is as powerful as somebody else saying it, especially the media. Your credibility and trust is heightened by the effects of a good public relations campaign.

Consider public relations as part of your marketing initiatives. If you don't understand this aspect of promoting your business, partner with someone who does.

If you are interested in finding out ways that you can create a positive buzz for your business, please visit our website at www.jjrmarketing.com

Do something proactive, pro-bono

Many companies donate to not-for-profit organizations, volunteer time or participate in special events in the community, but have you taken time to consider providing added-value to your clients? Surprising your clients with unexpected services or products at no charge can really make an impact on them. For example, a customer hired us to update their website content. As we worked on this project, we decided to incorporate social media integration at no additional charge. The customer was very pleased with our project and impressed with our added-value service. As a result, we have continued to work with that customer on many other projects. The key is to find something that stems from your expertise and doesn't cost you all that much, but provides a big benefit to the client. Little things go a long way!

Define one added-value benefit that you can create for one client this week:

Benefit: ______________________________________

Customer: ____________________________________

By when: _____________________________________

Understand multicultural marketing

Our communities are becoming more and more diverse. One of the largest and fastest growing segments of the United States is the Hispanic segment. Understanding this complex audience will be crucial as the organic growth continues to take place. This segment has incredible buying power. Companies that want to stay ahead of the game will learn the importance of creating specific campaigns that resonate with this group. Let's embrace diversity!

Learn about the Hispanic demographic.

When you are convinced that you need to market to this segment, partner with a multicultural expert that understands this growing segment of our population.

To learn more about marketing in a multicultural environment go to www.jjrmarketing.com.

Create a "viral" marketing effect

Often, we limit ourselves to things we can do physically. Creating viral marketing is important now because we live in a world where we no longer have to rely on the things we can do with our hands, but also with our minds. We can actually create a marketing machine in which we use the marketing and communication trends involving social media and text messaging. We take advantage of what is currently happening with the shift in the way we communicate with all these vehicles. When you are genuine and authentic and deliver a message that resonates with your audience, even if you only have 10 percent of audience members go out and tell five people about your amazing company, then those five people tell somebody else. That's one way we can create a viral affect. Another way to create a viral effect is by doing what I'm doing with this book, which is giving away a card and having readers text a keyword to the number on that card to listen to an introduction on their phone. This is something they can forward on to their friends, family, and colleagues. Using social media, I have advertised that the book is coming and to watch for it. By doing something similar, you will extend your arms to reach people who you never thought of reaching in the past. It is inexpensive, so you can reach more people with a lot less money. Create a message that resonates with your audience, use the vehicles you have access to for new marketing trends, and reach people you could never have imagined.

Get comfortable using viral marketing tools, such as text messages and social media. Make sure that the message resonates with the audience.

See how it unfolds before your eyes!

Forget about the state of the economy

We have been inundated with enough negativity, especially in recent years, as our economy has taken a turn for the worst. We get depressed and fearful we might become another victim. These feelings only paralyze us and keep us from moving forward. Take whatever steps you need to take, but never lose faith. As we entered this recession, I kept telling myself and others, "I will not participate in the recession. I am simply not interested." I certainly got a good laugh from people and a sense of hope, too. The good news is that regardless of what we are going through, we can create good opportunities if we only believe. And we did it! Our company grew 56 percent during one of the worst years of the economy. Yours can, too!

Write down three ideas you can employ to create opportunities during poor economic times:

Measure it

Whether you do a complex multi-channel integrated marketing campaign or a small project, it is important to measure the results. After all, if you can't measure results, why invest the time and resources to do it? There are a lot of ways you can measure marketing results, both direct and indirect. Some focus on return on investment (ROI), which has a direct impact on the bottom line, and some focus on return on objectives (ROO), which impacts the bottom line indirectly. For example, if you are hosting an event, your ROI goal is related to raising a certain amount of money. The ROO goal for the same event is to have a 75 percent attendance rate. This second goal is indirectly related to ROI on the surface, but it certainly affects it.

When you work on any marketing project or campaign for the next month, define:

ROI - what is the desired financial outcome of this campaign?

ROO - what are the objectives that you would like to meet for this campaign?

If you can't measure it, don't do it.

Section 4
Customer Retention

Customers are your most important asset. They are your gold mine. Taking care of them is extremely important. It takes 10 times more money and effort to find a new customer than to retain an existing one. These secrets will help you create an emotional connection with your customers so that you keep them for life.

Learn to say "NO" and maintain ethical standards

It is so difficult to maintain ethical standards at times. On one occasion, I had the opportunity to present to a big prospect. During the negotiation process, I noticed how the prospect was extremely demanding and that our ethical standards did not match. The money was great, but it did not feel right. I made the conscious decision to say "No" and walked away in a very polite and diplomatic way. By saying "No," I gained time and energy, and two days later, I landed two big clients that were nearly double the revenue.

It does not matter how big the client is. What matters is that it feels right to work with them. All of your emotional energy is maximized by working with clients who align with your ethical standards.

What steps can you take today to remove negative business relationships without burning any bridges?

You will become more productive, and your bottom line will increase.

Solve the problem first

In my years of marketing as an entrepreneur, I have come to understand that I need to think about how I can make a difference in the world of business with my services. Oftentimes people go into business thinking only of the money and instant gratification. If you open up your heart and try to solve the client's problems, those rewards – the perks, the money, everything else - will follow. You must focus on solutions for the client. In doing that, you will build a lasting relationship and have a client for life. That has been the case for a lot of our clients, and after several years, they still keep coming back to us.

I've been solving problems for clients for many years, even before I became an entrepreneur. You solve them by focusing on your client's objectives and goals rather than your own rewards. You do it by conducting assessments with your clients. You do it by taking time to meet with them and understanding what they're going through. Every time I get a new client, their problem becomes my problem. I take ownership of the issue, and I take credit and accountability for the success of solving the problem. The result is a happy ending. Taking this approach of solving the client's problems first, has been one of the most amazing things I can do for them. They feel cared for, they feel understood, and, most importantly, I see the tangible results that this approach delivers. This, of course, brings success because I have provided real solutions.

Create a needs assessment form that will allow you to identify the true needs of your clients.

Not what they say they want but what they need.

Create value through intellectual property

We all have an expertise. Creating value and a source of revenue is what I'm doing right now by writing this book. Information that is useful and can prove successful for other people can really be an inspiration for others. You, too, can capitalize on intellectual property, which is the knowledge and experience that is uniquely yours.

Take small steps, such as writing articles. By sharing that knowledge and experience, you create a reputation, and you create value for your clients. You can give them the peace of mind that they're working with someone who knows what they're talking about. The value can then be expanded to an additional stream of income. By creating value, you not only position yourself as an expert, you could also generate incremental revenue.

Create a product this week, whether it is an article, a blog, a report, or a speaking engagement, where you can share your knowledge and experience.

Opportunities to generate revenue will appear.

Create a process

People don't buy businesses; they buy the process. Ask yourself what the value of your business is; the value is the process. Large franchises have a formula or process that they follow. The success of any large company is not in the fact that their name is out there, but in the continuity and consistency of that company. The process that they follow allows people to expect consistency at every location. It's not always the product that they sell, but how they do it. Think about how you can make a difference in your business process. People sell processes; they sell formulas that are proven successful.

You must create a process to build expectations. When people know what to expect, they're more confident, and you get rid of the fear of the unknown.

Describe your process.

The most successful companies all have a process and a formula that they have created and followed.

Revise content before printing

It is so embarrassing to see incorrect content, whether it is misspelled, inaccurate, or wrongfully applied. How many thousands of dollars have been wasted in printing incorrect content? Every time I see something that is to be printed, I check and double-check to ensure that it is 100 percent correct, that graphics are high-quality, and that logos are properly displayed.

What two steps will you take today to revise content carefully before printing?

____

____

____

____

Proofreading content before investing money in printing can save you and your company a lot of money.

Communication, communication

Communication is a key element to any relationship. A good client relationship management program (CRM) can help you stay ahead of the game. For instance, I have a monthly newsletter that I send out to all of my contacts and clients. It ensures constant communication with them, and they begin to expect this type of communication at certain intervals. In addition, I contact them to request approval on pending action items by setting reminders. My clients are always impressed with this multi-touch approach. My motto is, "The ball is always in your court, and when it is in mine, it doesn't stay there long."

What do you do to stay in touch with your customers?

What types of initiatives do you engage in to stay in touch with your contacts?

What kind of communication would they like and find attractive?

Prove yourself with tangible results

Everyone wants to see results. Ensuring you can translate your actions into tangible results is critical in today's market. Be proactive in monitoring what your clients get from your company. The impact that your products or services make to a client might not be evident, but it is your job to define how that impact makes their life easier by improving processes or the bottom line. As you prove yourself with tangible results, you will see your business increase right before your eyes! Your reputation will be great, too!

Describe three recent results that you provided for your clients:

____

____

____

____

____

____

____

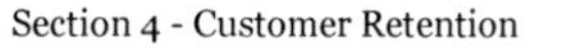

Stand out regardless of criticism

Many people settle into their life without any intention of getting out of their comfort zone to make a difference. Leaders are either born or made. And standing out from the crowd will likely get you noticed positively or generate jealousy. When you are paving the way for others, you become the center of attention and sometimes the recipient of criticism. Recognize why you are a leader, remember your vision, and refuse to let negative feedback influence you in any way. Go, leader, go!

Choose to stand out this week by doing something for somebody else.

You will create a positive buzz when your business community hears that you went out of your way to make a difference.

Remind your clients

Many times, our clients forget what we do for them, so it is important to remind them. As a general rule, I recap every project with my clients to ensure that the objectives were met. For example, I was once hired to create exposure for a local grocery store. After a three-month contract, I presented a summary of all the results and was able to identify the following: a 17 percent increase in revenues over the previous three years, a strong database had been created, and more than 1,200 new prospective clients walked through the store, (a 600-customer increase from previous years). Had we not summarized all these milestones, the client would not have appreciated our work as much. Taking the time to do this can strengthen a relationship and showcase the value you bring to your clients. After you showcase your success, it is important to ask for a testimonial.

My last success story with a client was:

____

____

____

____

____

____

____

____

Respect time

Time is our most precious asset, as it cannot be saved or retrieved. Being late to meetings or functions not only detracts from the purpose, but it also causes negative impressions, especially if it's the first or only time you are attending. It is rude to show up late because everyone's time is wasted, distractions are created, and the day's tasks fall behind for the rest of the day. If you are attending a meeting with five people and you are 10 minutes late, you have just wasted 50 minutes. Being on time, every time, will create a good impression and will show that you respect everyone's time.

Here are some things you can do this week to help you be on time for commitments and show that you respect people's time:

- *Plan ahead*
- *Create realistic time frames*
- *Set a goal to leave for appointments 15 minutes earlier than necessary*
- *Go to sleep on time*
- *Imagine a perfect morning*
- *Keep track of your time*
- *Set priorities*

100

Recognize your management style

There are several tools in the marketplace, such as personality assessments, that help you objectively define your personality traits and management style. They are cost-effective and efficient. Through these assessments, you can learn your work style, assess how you relate to other people in the workplace, and pinpoint what you enjoy most about your profession. Recognizing your management style will save you time, energy, and headaches. When you know your management style, you will be able to more effectively connect with your team to produce optimal results for your company. You will also be able to identify situations in which you can excel.

If you haven't already taken one, when will you take a personality assessment?_______________________________

If you have already assessed your skills, when will you review and apply the results?

____

Create a system to follow

We all follow a system or protocol, even in daily simple tasks. Take, for example, brushing your teeth: first you take the toothbrush, then apply toothpaste, proceed to brushing your teeth, and finally rinse. That is a system! After several meetings with prospects and clients, we developed the following steps for our marketing system:

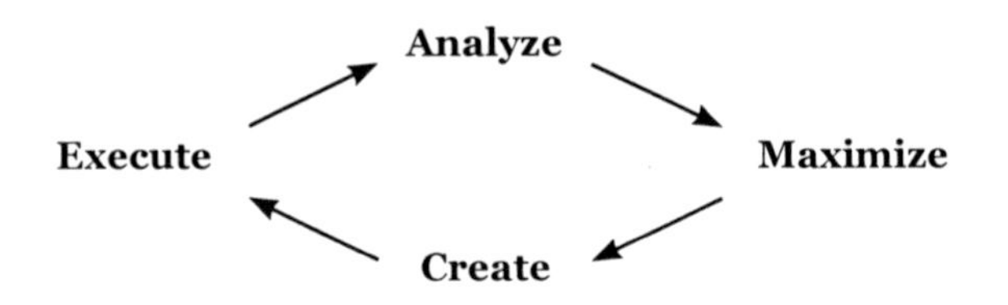

In the first step, we fully analyze what the client is currently doing for marketing and public relations by conducting a needs assessment session. In the second step, we maximize every current marketing/PR vehicle used by the client. In the third step, we create new marketing initiatives that resonate with the target audiences. In the fourth step, we execute the deliverables. This system becomes an ongoing practice that ensures client satisfaction every time. Developing a process will make you look more polished and professional and will impress your customers. In addition, it will make it easier for you and your staff to manage projects.

This week, begin documenting a system for your business.

You will notice a systematic approach to the activities you do every day.

Provide valuable information/education

Knowledge and experience are nothing if not shared with others. You can share your knowledge by creating reports, white papers, and articles. Speaking engagements are also a great way to share what you know with others. Doing this will slowly make you the go-to expert when other businesses or media are seeking more information about that particular topic. You will also get more leads and prospects for your business.

I will write ______________________________ this week

and will share it with: ______________________________

Never burn bridges

As a young girl, I learned from Dale Carnegie material that everything we ever do will be "with people, through people and for people." That statement was engraved in my head and has now been converted into a lifestyle for me. If this statement is true (which it is for me), this means that relationship management is key. In my many years of dealing with thousands of people, I have always made it a point to not only network, but to connect. At times, I have faced some negative people who were not willing to work with me. I have done my best to graciously walk away from those negative people, but there are times that this peaceful retreat is impossible. Never burn any bridges. Be honest and have the integrity to deal with negative people or situations.

What will you do this week to maintain your integrity in a bad situation?

Make sure the benefits outweigh the liability

When considering growing your business, it is easy to get excited about making decisions that might not have a sustainable foundation. Hiring new employees, buying a new machine, or expanding your office is exciting, but the benefits must be greater than the liability. For example, if you want to hire a new employee, make sure the value this person is bringing surpasses what you are paying. Evaluate each decision in your business to make sure it is backed by a solid list of benefits.

Write down the pros and cons of the decision you want to make:

PROS	*CONS*
______________________	______________________
______________________	______________________
______________________	______________________
______________________	______________________
______________________	______________________

Show your clients you appreciate them

When I started my business, I had a very small budget. Regardless of this, I always made it a point to invest in thank you cards and small gifts for my clients. Whether I buy lunch for their staff or send them flowers or chocolate-covered strawberries, I have shown and continue to show my appreciation for them. Doing this has helped me create not only clients for life, but friends as well.

List some clients who you will show your appreciation to this week:

1. ______________________________
2. ______________________________
3. ______________________________
4. ______________________________
5. ______________________________

Enjoy a good family or personal vacation

Business owners who don't take time to rest and rejuvenate are not performing at the top level. When you do, it is important that you really enjoy it. I am a workaholic and was in a rut because I didn't think about taking family vacations. But when we took our first family vacation with our 2-year-old, it was amazing. Not only did it allow me to see things objectively, but it also allowed me to put things on hold and just enjoy spending time with my family. When I came back, it was exciting to say, "I am so grateful that I have a business, that I am doing what I love every day, and that I had this time to refresh and renew so I could come back and do even more amazing things." Taking a good vacation helps you relax and helps you appreciate the things you have back home. It brings you an amazing feeling of being refreshed and renewed and gives you more energy to conquer the world.

I am taking my next vacation on ____________, and I am leaving my computer at home.

Recharge!

Recognize success NOW

Success is not a one-time event but a series of progressive steps that get you closer to your goals. Where you are NOW is a step toward success; it is getting closer to the goal that you are trying to achieve. Having a keen sense of awareness of success now is so important, because that fuels your motivation. It lets you know that you are closer to reaching your goals and your objectives. You are successful along every step of the process. You don't have to wait until three years from now when you reach your ultimate goal. By taking small steps today and by getting closer to your objective, you are successful now. You may may feel at times like you are not doing anything and not getting close because you are still three or four years away from your goal. But the actions that you take every day, and the constant motivation that you apply to your life, make you successful now.

I like to write down my accomplishments, visualizing the steps and feeling the sense of accomplishment now. A great example is writing this book. I knew the book was going to be finished someday. At times, however, I felt like I had so much to do to accomplish this.

Be aware that the steps you are taking to get closer to your goal make you successful now. It is going to fuel your motivation; keep you on track, keep you going.

Write down your goal: ______________________________

____

____

Recognize two steps that you have accomplished toward this goal:

1. ____

2. ____

Reward yourself for accomplishing these steps.

Set up a tracking mechanism for your goals.

Enjoy the process!

Constantly evolve

We are afraid to change. But by constantly evolving, we make progress on our goals and in our lives. It is important to stay abreast of what is going on, to recognize change is happening, and to embrace the change.

I worked for a grocery store that had been around for about 83 years. This was a third generation store that had been doing things the same old way for many, many years. What I really admired about this client is that when I presented them with a new marketing plan to take advantage of new approaches in the marketplace, they opened up to change. We were able to employ new marketing strategies, such as text messaging, for somebody who had been doing things for so many years the same way. They did not even know how to send a text message, but they were open to it. This was completely innovative, and it really portrayed the evolution of the times and how we can use immediate communication. It is important to always be willing to evolve. You are able to maximize the opportunities you have to go to the next level in your business.

Identify one area that can be improved:

____

____

____

Do it!

Get rid of negativity

We let ourselves be swayed by what we see physically or by circumstances. A positive attitude allows you to change that and allows you to not compromise your attitude about what you see but rather by how you react to the circumstances. We see negativity all the time and let ourselves become involved in that negativity. Why is it important to get rid of it? Because it leaves us more prone to success. In addition, we create an environment of positivity that attracts other people. Do not get involved in a negative situation.

Think of a negative situation that you are in right now and define one way you can turn that into a positive.

When you are positive, you become a light for people around you and they expect that from you.

Embrace "servant leadership"

Humility is the way to lead. You can lead by example, not by a forced, push-it-down-your-throat type of approach. I attended an event where a hospital CEO was presenting this concept, telling how he applies servant leadership and how we, as leaders, are servants. We are not here to be served but we are here to serve others. A couple of years before I went to this presentation, I survived a near-death experience. As I came out of the surgery, the doctor told my brother that he did not know if I was going to survive. I remember later, I was looking at the ceiling of the hospital asking myself, "Why did God give me another chance? What am I here to do?" Something that came to mind over and over again was that I was here to serve other people. That is my mission: I feel it in my heart, and I feel it in every inch of my body. I am here to serve. I am here to make a name that means service. I know that one way to lead people is by an example of service.

By being yourself and by being a servant, you are authentic and genuine, and the vibes you create are incredible. All you have to do is be willing to serve, and anything else will come to you. I have seen that. I am genuine to my mission in life. Every time I have a meeting with someone, I ask myself how I can bring value. This is one of the first questions I ask every single person I meet. How can I serve you? How can we be of assistance? It's not from the standpoint of getting business, but genuinely from the standpoint of serving people. If I focus on that, everything else inevitably comes.

Which service gesture can you perform today?

☐ *Share a connection*

☐ *Pick up the phone and ask, "Can I help you with something today?"*

☐ *Donate your time to a local group*

☐ *Other:* ____

Don't take it personally

People tend to take things personally in business sometimes. As passionate as you are about your job or your profession, it is important to stand back and be objective. This could be the difference between getting and not getting a client. They may make a comment to you and you begin to react, thinking they are attacking you when their comment is just an observation about the business. Do not take things personally; it has nothing to do with you.

They have provided information. You need to analyze it and view it as feedback. It is not about you. When people give you this kind of feedback, do not get emotionally tied to it.

List a negative situation and the feedback you were given. Put your feelings aside, and ask yourself if the statement is valid. Ask the question, "What can I do to make sure this does not happen again?"

Remember, things are often said that have nothing to do with you personally. Knowing this will save you headaches and help you stay objective in business.

Spend time strategizing your own company

We are so objective about somebody else's company, especially as consultants. The problem is we get so inundated with the day-to-day operations that we forget to strategize and look at our own company. Strategizing from time to time, assessing your goals and reviewing what you are doing with your own business could greatly accelerate your success and can help you maximize every opportunity.

Set some time aside away from the office to specifically think about your business objectively.

Current state of my business:

____

____

Goals:

____

____

Opportunities:

____

____

Next action items:

____

____

Define your strengths

How many times do we focus on the negative, and the things we do not have? The strength in your business, even if you work for somebody else, is your unique selling proposition. You do not have to be a jack of all trades. You do not have to be everything to everyone. But if you can define your strength in your areas of opportunity, this could be huge. Find your strengths, and feature those unique propositions in bold, prominent bullet points on your website, every collateral piece, any mailing piece, and any marketing campaign. The strength of your business and your unique selling propositions are the reasons why people come to you. Define your strengths, and capitalize on them. Doing this will help you succeed, save you time, money, and energy, and positions you as an expert.

Define five unique selling propositions:

Narrow it down to the top three:

1. ______________________________
2. ______________________________
3. ______________________________

Allocate them in every customer touchpoint.

These are the reasons why people come to you!

114

Learn to delegate

You have to learn to delegate in order to succeed. You must focus on the things you can do and then let other people focus on the things you cannot do or you do not have time to do. Find people who can help you achieve your goals. If you hold on to that micromanage mentality, you are never going to achieve anything. You are only going to be able to achieve the things you can physically do. I am a perfectionist. I like to do things myself to make sure they are perfect and done the exact way I want them done. But I learned that there are people who have something to contribute. Maybe they do not have the skills or the experience that you have. If you let go and train other people to help you, then you are creating a much bigger force than what you can physically do by yourself.

What are some things that only you can do?

___

___

___

Now, what are three things that you can delegate?

___

___

___

Focus on what matters most

Oftentimes, we focus on the little things that do not have an impact, and they tend to take more energy than the big-picture things. You can delegate the small things in order to focus on what matters the most for your business. You do not need to be doing data entry; that is something you can delegate to somebody else. You can instead focus on preparing a presentation for a client, meeting with a prospect, or doing a speaking engagement. Focusing on the big things can have an effect on your business operation and your overall bottom line. By managing the chain of command and employing subcontractors who can do the work for you, you can focus on what matters most, which is bringing in more clients and, ultimately, more revenue. This can make an impact on the bottom line, and it can energize you and your business.

What are the two most important things in your business?

1. ______________________________
2. ______________________________

Here is a sample list:

- *Business development*
- *Customer service*
- *Deliverables*
- *Quality*
- *Marketing*
- *Referrals*

Focus on these!

116

Employ an easy-to-manage database

Many businesses do not have a systematic process for collecting data and using that data effectively. You can maximize the opportunity you have to communicate with the people around you by creating reminders, traces, or regular communications. The objective is to have a process that is easy and does not take away from the business. You have a lot of setup in the beginning, but in the long run it will save you time. It also allows you to create an emotional connection, as if you were there, because the communication is in your own words and phrases. It is automating the process of communication, which keeps things from falling through the cracks, keeps things moving in the right direction.

Research client relationship management (CRM) options, and employ the one that best works for you, based on your budget and specific situation.

CRM Comparison

Options	Price	Key Benefits
1		
2		
3		

CRM will save you a lot of time.

Use time wisely

We waste time doing unnecessary things that are urgent but not important. You must schedule time for your family and find ways to manage tasks. The goal is to eliminate stress and still feel like you are on top of things. Develop a system of answering your e-mails and telephone calls to avoid being overwhelmed and stressed out.

Create your own rules about how you use your time:

Voicemail:

____

____

E-mails:

____

____

Family time:

____

____

Other:

____

____

118

Take a customer-centric approach

What you say is not necessarily what your customers want. Work on finding out and getting to the core and the depth of that relationship, and finding out what moves your customers. Do not let yourself dictate what those things are without having that empirical data from surveys or from asking direct questions to your customers. You must give the customer what they want: something that is affordable, somebody to take control, and somebody to hold them accountable and take them to the next level. Create an emotional connection with the customer, and you will have repeat business and gain referrals.

What questions can you ask customers in a survey?

1. ______________________________
2. ______________________________
3. ______________________________
4. ______________________________
5. ______________________________

What can you change in your business model to adjust to the findings of your survey?

Make it all about them!

119

Time cannot be stored

Time is of the essence to accomplish our tasks and maximize our resources. We waste our time on the little things that do not matter. Have a daily routine to maximize your time. You can make lists and set up multiple meetings. If you are organized, you can find time to do the things you want to do. By taking charge of your time, you'll feel more relaxed and energized.

For the next week, each night before you go to bed, visualize your next day, from the time you awaken until the time you go to bed. Then make a list of action items for that next day.

120

Take the referrals you can handle

Don't spread yourself too thin. Sometimes with referrals, we feel as if we're obligated to take them because somebody we trust and appreciate sends us that client. You're always going to have referrals, and you must do a good job, not just for the referral but for the person who referred them to you. Learn to say no if you can't help them. If you're unable or unwilling to take the referral, you still have the responsibility to phone the referring customer or send an e-mail to tell them you appreciate the referral but you can't assist them. The person who referred you will appreciate your honesty!

Follow up on every referral. Use your process to filter through the ones that will work and won't work.

121

A good leader and communicator

According to Ed Horn, the 2006 Toastmasters World Champion, **C**oaching, **C**hallenge to step forward, and **C**ommitment to excellence - are the three ingredients for a successful speech. If you are a good leader and a good communicator, you are going to be successful in whatever you do. If you can effectively communicate with people and inspire them, you can do anything you want and be successful in any field. You will gain more business and more credibility. You will experience a true connection because of the way you are presenting yourself. You are going to create that viral effect and gain third-party endorsements. That translates into an opportunity: you being in front of a captive audience that wants to hear from you.

Find a local Toastmasters Club and attend as a guest.

For more information, visit www.toastmasters.org

122

Have regular meetings

We are often so inundated throughout our day-to-day operations that we forget to have regular meetings with our staff. You need to work and strategize regularly, so schedule meetings where you give a state of your business and assign or review action steps for employees.

Have regular meetings. Discuss what items are important to the staff, and list three of those items.

Discuss these 3 components in staff meetings:

- *Past items*
- *Current items*
- *Action items*

Organize yourself

Disorganization causes you to lose time, energy, and customers. Find and stick with whatever type of organization works for you. I have a file for each customer, and everything pertaining to that customer goes in the file in chronological order. I constantly stay organized by answering e-mails and creating lists. Use resources and tools to stay organized, which can save you time and energy. It can also help you stay ahead of action items. As a result, you have a more efficient workplace, and your productivity goes up.

Do you have an organizational system in place, such as a filing system?

Say to yourself, "This week I will organize ______________*."*

Always confirm meetings ahead of time

Diligently confirming meetings will save you time. How long did you spend traveling in your car, only to find out that the client was not available even though you set up a specific time for that meeting? A simple call or an e-mail to confirm will not only help you stay ahead of the game, but will also impress your customer and maximize the use of your time.

Have you confirmed all meetings this week?

☐ *Yes*

☐ *No*

Maximize networking connections

Networking is not just about meeting people, but creating an emotional connection. If you focus on giving, before receivng, the end result will be positive. Remember to connect with people by making them feel important. For example, you can contact your existing connections and introduce them to new people, send them a gift, comment on a hobby, among others. *Be authentic, and be willing to give before you receive.*

Below, are the six steps that Brian Marshall created to turn your network into a referral machine:

1. *Make contact*
2. *Identify the introductions to make*
3. *Coach the connection*
4. *Make the connection*
5. *Help others help you*
6. *Receive introductions*

Download the complete process at:
www.bizsecretsthatwork.com/referralmachine.pdf

Start using it today.

126

Show the savings

Customers love to see how much money they are saving. They do not necessarily care about how much they are spending if they can see the value, but they do care about how much they are going to save. If you can give the client a discount, giving them more value, they will focus on the savings rather than what they are paying. Every business, large or small, is concerned about how they can stretch their dollars. Always show savings on their invoice as a line item; when you deliver the product or the service, they will be extremely happy to see they are saving money.

Define one way you can showcase savings and add value for your customers.

___

___

___

Extend your arms

Extending your arms means recognizing that you are not alone and that you can only do so much on your own. It means getting out of your comfort zone and making a difference in your family, business, and community. Whether it is to help or to receive help, there are many people that have been there and can help you on your journey. Connecting with people who are aligned with your vision can be the difference between making a real impact in the world or not.

How will you extend your arms this week to:

Give: ______________________________

Receive: ____________________________

Extend your arms today!

Create a pricing structure that works for your clients

Creating a pricing structure is about knowing the marketplace, your customers, and your prospects, and giving them what they want while staying true to your goals. Be flexible to accommodate your clients but keep your business profitable. Create a pricing structure that works for all parties involved. Having flexibility will allow you to create more incremental revenue for your business!

Select one that you are currently not using, and explore it as an option:

- ☐ *Retainers*
- ☐ *Projects*
- ☐ *Hourly rates*
- ☐ *Bundle packages*
- ☐ *Automatic credit card options*

Provide options!

Your treasure: clients

There is no business success without clients. They are your treasure! Because your clients are your most valuable asset, you must protect and take care of them. Thousands of dollars are spent on client acquisition, when reaching out to your existing clients can provide you more success. When your clients are satisfied, they become a catalyst for more business opportunities. It takes 10 times more money and effort to get a new client than to keep an existing one. You can take care of your treasure by delivering value, and by caring, listening, showing appreciation, going the extra mile, etc.

What will you do this week to take care of your clients?

____

____

____

____

____

Remember, your clients are your gold mine.

Leave it at home

We all have personal issues. However, keeping them home is a good idea, much like the saying, "What happens in Vegas, stays in Vegas."

You have a responsibility as a business owner or professional to show your best face at all times. Your audience does not deserve to hear about your negative experiences. Don't let negative personal situations affect the business. It doesn't matter what happens to you; it's how you handle it. Don't dwell on your problems. Instead of being a victim, find solutions so that you can present your best self.

Never bring your negative, personal situations into the business world. Don't complain, especially in front of prospective clients. You must be objective and think what an effect this could have on your client. It's tempting to talk about the negative, but if you can avoid it, your life will turn more positive!

This week, try not to complain in front of a prospect, client, or a colleague.

Show your best self, and leave the problems at home.

Section 5
Motivation

Motivation is intrinsic. It cannot be transferred from person to person on a consistent basis. We must generate motivation from inside in order for it to be sustainable and long lasting. The following secrets will help you stay on track and will be a source of motivation each time you decide to open up this book.

Be yourself

Being true to yourself is the epitome of success. When you try to please somebody else, you find yourself lacking that sense of accomplishment and happiness because you're trying to be somebody you are not. Capitalize on what you are, and accept yourself for who you are. You can achieve everything you want by being authentic, accepting who you are, and capitalizing on the things that make you unique.

Define the traits that make you who you are.

____

____

____

____

____

For the next week, try to turn those traits into opportunity.

Focus on the prize

We have so many distractions: tempting job offers, others who don't support us, new ideas, housework, and many others. When I started my company, I had a vision to be a successful entrepreneur and make a difference for other businesses. Because initially, I did not have an exact road map, there were a lot of temptations to give up or to forget why I even started the business. Every time I was tempted, I would reconnect by reminding myself of my vision and dream.

Write your vision for your business or your ultimate prize here:

____

____

____

____

List the distractions in your life that make it difficult to focus:

____

____

____

____

Each time one of those distractions comes to you, read your vision and you will overcome any temptations. Focus on your prize!

Remember you can achieve ANYTHING you want

Many people launch dreams, but they never attain them. It's not because they do the work, but because when it was time to receive the reward, they doubted. As a young entrepreneur, I can remember many times when I doubted whether I could achieve my dreams. During those times, I always reminded myself that I could do anything as long as I stayed true to myself. Put your dreams in writing, look at them every day, and take small steps every day to attain them.

What steps are you taking today to help you get closer to your dream?

____

____

____

____

When you are approaching your dream, what will you do to embrace it?

____

____

____

____

Be open to new ideas and inspiration

Ideas are ideas. Inspiration is an idea with a good feeling. You have to pay special attention to the latter since they are the tools that propel your success. I created an "idea log" where I capture the date, subject, and brilliance for each idea I have. This tool lets me capture those thoughts that wander around in my mind and make them tangible. They help me feel energized, in control of life, and, of course, become the driver of my destiny.

Oftentimes, we are not open to being the recipient of ideas. Follow your heart and mind when you feel inspired. By using this process you can convert ideas and inspiration into actions.

Be open to inspiration that you get today.
Write it down, analyze it, and take action.

See how you feel!

Achieving your dreams feels AMAZING!

Keeping a journal is helpful in the success of this secret. Write in your journal every day how things are going and how you dealt with issues. At the end of the week, write a summary of your accomplishments for the week. Then take time to read your journal. This exercise will help you to realize that you are achieving your dreams.

Knowing you've conquered a dream and that you are living the physical manifestation of your dream makes you stronger, and prone to achieving more in the future. It gives you confidence to proceed to the next step. It also helps you realize you deserve and can have anything you want. By journaling, you see that you have a dream, you are working towards the dream, and you will obtain that dream. You can create, and have everything you want. Being in the present moment, journaling about your small victories, can keep you in a state of bliss every day.

Close your eyes and feel the attainment of your dreams. Describe as many details as possible and write them down in your journal.

What clothes are you wearing? Where are you? Who is there with you? This is a very powerful exercise.

Magically enough, when you do obtain those dreams they will unfold before your eyes exactly the way you envisioned them.

Never give up

How many times have you gone through a stressful situation and decided to give up at the first opportunity? Anyone can embark on a new dream, but it can be difficult to maintain the dream. We are tempted by internal and external factors that can cause us to simply let go of our dreams. Stay focused.

Staying focused is what keeps you going. If you stay positive, anything you desire can come true. You may have deadlines, or you may be tired or sick, but don't give up. You must visualize the results. Reaching your dream will be the greatest reward. What will you do today to reinforce your dream?

Write down a goal that you're working on:

____

____

____

Visualize the completion of that goal, and see how it feels to have it in your hands.

Do this at least twice a day.

Create a mastermind group

Not having the support you need might be detrimental to your success. A mastermind group will give you that support and help you identify the things that drive and motivate you from within. It is so important to align yourself with people who have the same values as you. You can use their resources and knowledge to create the mastermind group, and learn from them. The idea is that we are all built with an inner guidance system that allows us to make decisions and choices in our lives. Through the engagement of a mastermind group you can tap into those answers and make them a reality. The answers have always been there inside of you.

This concept helps you define who you are as an individual. You'll find answers to things you probably would not have found if you were not tapping into yourself. We go outside looking for answers, but when you have a mastermind group, you can dig deeply into who you are and find the answers to everything you want.

Do research this week about what a mastermind group is and write it down below:

What is a mastermind group?

____

____

____

____

____

Are you ready to be part of one?

Define the commitment

Commitment is the root of success. Without commitment, you will not achieve anything. You must be extremely committed, which can be scary, but commitment creates sustainability and a foundation to achieve anything you want. Commitment allows you to convert something non-tangible into something tangible. When you feel like you are sliding away from where you want to be, take some sort of action that gets you back on track.

Look at the actions that you are facing in the next seven days. Pick something that is important but not urgent, and do that.

What will you do this week that is important, but not urgent?

____

____

____

Know what you want

Sometimes we don't know what we want in life. You have options because of the skills, talents, and abilities that you possess, and you are the one who gets to give yourself permission to uncover or rediscover the things that you love doing. Define your passion. What is it you want? It is okay to ask questions, such as "Why am I not happy? Why can't I find my passion?" As you seek, the questions will be answered.

Write down what you want from life. If you knew there were no limitations, what would you want for your life?

____

____

____

____

____

____

There are no limitations!

140

Perseverance and persistence are key

We all start projects. In fact, we might start several projects at one time, but not complete them. When I was in high school, I decided to start writing diaries and promised myself to write every single day, no matter what, for one year. This small test proved to be one of my biggest challenges. Sometimes I was out of town, sick, or simply did not feel like writing. Regardless, I kept writing every single day for one year, two months, and six days; then I realized that I had gone beyond my commitment, which made me feel great. This challenge helped me understand the importance of commitment. I knew that by accomplishing this task, I would have the tools to persevere in bigger challenges. I apply this mentality to my business and to everything I do in other areas of my life.

Commit yourself to something this month, whether it is starting an exercise program, writing a book, creating a process, or something else you want to achieve.

I commit to:

____

____

____

____

141

Recap your success from time to time

As we get busy in our lives, both personally and professionally, we oftentimes forget our accomplishments, which might cause us to feel bad or exhausted. In order to stay motivated, I write down my accomplishments at least once a month. When I am having a difficult day, I reflect back on my business journal; after reading it, I feel a sense of excitement and energy. If you have succeeded in the past, you can continue to duplicate those experiences.

When was the last time you sat down to recap your successes and achievements?

____

Write down five great things that happened to you over the past month:

1. ____
2. ____
3. ____
4. ____
5. ____

Use gratitude as a way of living

This is probably one of the most important things you can do to be successful. If you are not grateful for what you have currently, how do you expect to receive better things in the future? Be grateful for everything you have, starting with your family, home, car, clothes, food, job, or business. Don't take things for granted. When you begin to feel gratitude in your heart, you will see more of those great things coming to you unexpectedly. Gratitude accelerates your dreams and desires.

List five things that you are grateful for:

*I am grateful now that I*______________________________

____

*I am grateful now that I*______________________________

____

*I am grateful now that I*______________________________

____

*I am grateful now that I*______________________________

____

*I am grateful now that I*______________________________

____

Vision, motivation, perseverance & resiliency

These four things are the reasons for my success. Vision has given me the ability to see beyond what is in front of me. Motivation has propelled that vision and given me a burning desire for the possibilities of what I can create with that vision. Perseverance has given me the constant energy to back up motivation. And resiliency has given me the strength not to give up in a difficult situation.

What is your vision? ______________________________

____

____

____

What motivates you about this vision? ______________

____

____

____

What action can you take today toward this vision? ____

____

____

____

What can you do to overcome obstacles that keep you from this vision? ______________________________

____

____

____

Think BIG

We sometimes limit ourselves to little things when we shouldn't. My mentor Jerry Mitchell once told me, "Think big, think big! Why limit yourself when you have the world?" You can change the world by thinking big.

When I embark on a new project, I think of his words, and I'm open to the possibilities instead of constrained by a tiny little project. I try to think about how what I am doing can grow to become national or international. You will receive rewards that you never believed possible just by thinking of the big things that you can accomplish and by having a mission.

List some things you can change in your business model to adjust to a bigger picture:

____

____

____

____

____

____

____

Think BIG!

Help without expecting anything in return

One of the noblest ways we can make an impact in the world is by giving. Whether you give time, money, or resources, give them without expecting anything in return. I make this a part of my life. For example, if a friend is looking for a job, I go out of my way to connect her with people who can help. If a local business is having an event, I go out of my way to get the information in my newsletter, which reaches more than 5,000 readers. You notice a trend here? Go out of your way to help. Get out of your comfort zone to make an impact in other people's lives.

Who will you help this week?

____

____

How will you go out of your way to help him or her?

____

____

Apply learning lessons every day

Learning and applying new lessons in our lives makes us grow and gain new insights. I have expertise in marketing and PR, but I never stop applying new things I learn. For example, when a new report on marketing statistics comes out, I read it and begin incorporating the statistics (as supporting facts) into my client presentations.

You can convert something non-existent to something that exists, something successful, just by applying it. Similarly, you can take a proven method or idea from someone and incorporate it into your life and apply it immediately.

What have you learned this week?

___

___

___

Have you applied it?

☐ *Yes*

☐ *No*

147

Remember your passion when times get stressful

Nobody said that the road to success would be easy. It is important to remember that you love what you do during difficult times. On a handful of occasions, I was ready to pull my hair out because of frustration or stress. Instead, I took a deep breath and analyzed why I was feeling like that. I remembered all the amazing people I meet every day and how much I enjoy doing what I do. I visualized the faces of appreciation and love. Then I realized that we all have difficult times, and that is when it's most important to reconnect with what we love. Always be aware of your passion in your profession so that when the going gets tough, you will be able to move on with enthusiasm.

What part of your profession do you enjoy the most?

____

____

____

Create abundance

The "Law of Circulation" states that whatever you give returns to you tenfold or more. This law is unbreakable, just like the "law of gravity." Create an abundance of knowledge, experiences, and assets, and share them with others around you. I share my newsletter, contacts, and information with business professionals on an ongoing basis and receive incredible support back from them. There is enough to go around for everyone, and the more you make tangible and non-tangible things circulate, the more you will receive. It's the law.

List one tangible or non-tangible attribute or asset that you can share with someone this week:

Who will you share it with?

Get motivated

Let's face it: we live in a negative world. We all have bad days, but we always have the option to turn the day around and make it amazing. Every time I answer the phone and somebody asks me, "How are you?" my answer is always, "Amazing!" I will confess that I am not amazing all the time, but I get motivated by the phone calls I receive and just saying that every time changes my state of mind. On the other side of the phone, the affect is wonderful. I have received many compliments from people about my positive attitude. Motivation is also measured by your commitment to doing what is not necessarily urgent, but important. Choose to do tasks, even if you don't feel like it, and you will begin to see the difference in your motivation level. Getting motivated and sharing it with others builds genuine relationships. Your motivation is increased every time you light the way for somebody else.

What do you do every day to get motivated?

____

____

____

Stand firm in the face of adversity

Being a young Hispanic female made me plenty vulnerable. Just months into my business, I worked with a client whose financial situation took a negative turn, and he decided that he wouldn't pay me. I was devastated and debated for a long time whether I had done something wrong, but I could not find any reason for his excuse not to pay. Months went by, and I still anguished over what to do, knowing that I had the results to prove my success. I decided to stand firm in my conviction that I had done a good job and took legal action. The lawsuit was a victory, and I had my money sooner than I expected.

Are you facing adversity? ☐ Yes ☐ No
How can you apply this secret in your life today to ensure that you remain firm?

____

____

____

Don't give up; you are worth it!

Feed your burning desire

Your burning desire is the driver of your dreams. It is the non-tangible, non-visible intrinsic force that makes you do all the things you do every day. Feeding your burning desire with goals and objectives to keep you moving forward is key. I constantly meditate, read, and visualize my dreams as if they are already here. Thinking about this excites me and motivates me to keep moving. We all have an inner guidance system that allows us to ensure we are doing the right things. The burning desire inside of us lets us know if we are on track by how we feel. When you feed your burning desire, you will begin to turn your life from ordinary to extraordinary.

What creates excitement for you? What makes the fire in your belly grow?

___

___

___

Try these methods to take your burning desire to the next level this week:

- *Meditate*
- *Write down your dreams*
- *Visualize*
- *Feel what it is like to have your dreams here now*

Pay it forward

There are many local organizations that need your help. Whether it is sharing your experience with others, mentoring students, or stocking food, we can all spare a little bit of time to make a difference in our community. You will feel great knowing that you helped make the world a better place for you and those around you.

Name two organizations that you can contribute to this week:

1. ______________________________

2. ______________________________

Be aware of amazing opportunities

In the book *The Secret*, author Rhonda Byrne proposes a three-step process for using the "Law of Attraction" to achieve your dreams. These steps are: ask, believe, and receive. Being aware of opportunities references the third step in this process. We work so hard for our goals and objectives, but when we are about to receive, we might become skeptical. Every day, maintain a keen sense of awareness of possible opportunities. Staying aware will make you happy, knowing that you are taking advantage of the opportunities around you.

Are you ready to receive?

☐ *Yes* ☐ *No*

List one good opportunity that you can take advantage of this week:

____

____

____

154

Innovate and create

Your business can't survive without constant innovation. You have to stay aware of new marketing and business trends, and adjust to the cyber world that we live in. You must innovate, or you will fail.

I do this by listening to my clients and the people around me. 2009 was one of the most difficult years for a lot of businesses. In fact, a lot of them went out of business, and many barely made it. My innovation came into play when we saw small businesses suffer; they were losing market share, and I became disillusioned to see it happening. Even though we went through a rough patch ourselves, we survived by being innovative and creative. We came up with a small business marketing report that we priced very affordably. We created an economic stimulus marketing seminar where we provided marketing basics for business owners to go along with the marketing report. We ended up doing a series of three seminars throughout the year in conjunction with the local chamber of commerce. This project was one of the reasons why our growth margin and gross profits from 2008 to 2009 were up 56 percent during one of the worst economic times in years. Had we not been innovative, listened to what the marketplace was telling us, and changed accordingly, we probably wouldn't have achieved that growth.

Listen to the marketplace to adjust to changes and shifts in the paradigm, especially now in the cyber era. Do not be afraid to get out of your comfort zone. Be an innovator, be the first one to apply technology, be the first one to combine technologies for your clients.

Move to a place that is uncomfortable (in front of the product curve).

List some things that you might be afraid to change:

____

____

____

____

____

Remember, you stay in business by constantly innovating.

Seek knowledge

When I was just seven years old, I was exposed to incredible literature from Dale Carnegie (*How to Win Friends and Influence People*), Napoleon Hill (*Think and Grow Rich*), and Zig Ziglar (*Inspiration*), among many others. Now an adult, I continue to seek motivation, self-help, and other information to help me stay ahead. The more I know, the more I want to learn. Information is available at libraries, online, in magazines and newspapers, and from many other sources. Seeking knowledge will help you stay current and useful.

What will you do today to learn something new?

____

____

____

Positive attitude: always see the bright side

Have you heard "the half-full, half-empty cup" anecdote? An optimistic person sees the cup half-full while to the pessimist, it is half-empty. We all have difficult situations, obstacles, hardships, and challenges, but we also have the ability to reach out in a positive way and turn them into learning lessons. It is very easy to be positive when things are going well, but the true test comes when we face a difficult situation. When you begin to feel a glimpse of negativity, IMMEDIATELY make the conscious and clear choice to shift those thoughts to positive replacements.

When you are in the middle of a difficult situation this week, STOP for a moment and think of a positive experience (personal or professional). Begin to feel the happiness. Notice how the negative situation suddenly turns into something very small and disappears.

That's where the magic begins!

Embrace life

Life is so precious! I love the physical things in my life, but I also love that I am alive. Many people go through life without appreciating the little things, often taking them for granted. Why focus on trivial things? Why not focus on the essence of life? Be grateful for what you have because it could be gone tomorrow. By focusing on all the great blessings in your life, you can be happier and more fulfilled.

Make a list of all the little things in your life that you are grateful for: family, friends, home, vehicle, etc. For the next 24 hours, observe and pay close attention to all the little things that make your life easier.

____

____

____

____

____

You will be more alert and grateful and more things will come to you!

Take away emotion from business

People often take things personally in business. Business is business, regardless of your emotions, and not being able to separate the two might be detrimental to your success.

For example, I had that customer suddenly decide not to pay me even though I had done everything right. I had only been in business for a few months and felt taken advantage of. That was detrimental to my development at that time because I would come home and cry about it. That emotion caused suffering inside of me, and it also caused me not to work as effectively as I could have. It did not allow me to see things objectively, which is what emotion will do to you.

After fighting with this for weeks, I said, "You know what? I just cannot let this emotion take over. I have to step back and look at this objectively."

After I took away the emotions, I decided to take legal action and represented myself. I think that was one of the more important milestones in my business because I stood up for myself. Yes, I felt vulnerable; yes, I felt taken advantage of. Those emotions were hurting me, but I stopped and said, "I cannot continue like this. I have to take action."

Taking away the emotions can propel you toward success. It can take you to the next level. Because you are going to see things clearly and objectively, you can move on.

How can you apply objectivity to your business today?

Keep your promises

I have found people in my career who have said they would send me something or contact me about something. Weeks went by and nothing ever happened. I always ended up following up with them with a courtesy reminder. So, now I make it a point to do what I say I am going to do.

People I know in business generally do what they say they are going to do when they say they are going to do it. I am not saying that the rest of them don't, but they don't do it in a timely manner, or I have to remind them to do it.

Every time I go to a meeting and say I am going to do something, I write down those things I said I would do using key words. If I am going to a networking event and I don't have a pen to write with, I take the upper right hand corner of a business card and I fold it in. Then when I get back to the office, and notice that some of the cards are folded, I know that there is an action item attached to that card. I immediately take action and get it done, and I feel a sense of accomplishment. The person was expecting it and now will get it. I have received so many comments from people saying, "You know Jackie, you are on top of things. When you say you are going to do something, you do it." This impresses people, which is important in business. Keep your promises!

When you are out and about this week make one small promise and keep it.

You will feel wonderful!

Be your best self

By trying to keep up with the expectations of the world, you are alienating yourself from who you are. You must be yourself. This is the only way you can achieve true success. It is okay to be yourself and to love yourself. The day you accept yourself for what you are and who you are is the day you will be able to achieve success. Do not let others dictate to you what your life should be. Be your best self!

Decide what you like about yourself:

____

____

____

____

____

For the next 100 years, strive to be your best self!

Remain humble

There is no sustainable success without humility. When you reach success and attain the respect of people, you will lose everything if you are self-absorbed. True success comes from a foundation of humility, making your way in the world without blowing your own whistle. Maintain an open attitude toward acknowledging a higher power. When you are humble and authentic, your impact will be far greater than you ever dreamed. Humility is a willingness to serve and to make a difference in the world. Put yourself on the other side, do something for other people, and serve.

Take time this week to go to a nursing home or assisted living home to speak with the elderly. They have so much wisdom and can teach you so much.

Support from family and friends

There is no success without family support. Sometimes we leave our family behind when we go out to pursue our careers, but true success comes from the support of others. You do not have to be married or have kids to be successful but success comes with somebody in the background cheering you on, somebody backing you up. With family or friends supporting you, you will achieve success.

Find a family member or a friend who encourages and supports you, someone with whom you can share your progress and life experiences.

Who is that person?

___

Just having somebody to share things with is huge.

Get out of your comfort zone

We are sometimes too comfortable with what we have in our life and complain about what we don't have. Doing something that is not urgent, but important, is the same thing as getting out of your comfort zone. The objective is to get beyond what you are comfortable doing, to challenge yourself to be better than you normally are so you grow just a little bit more.

What is it that you have avoided doing? Do something today that is going to move you forward even if it's uncomfortable. The one thing that you are putting off is still going to be as ugly at the end of the day as it was at the beginning of the day. Find one thing that you are not doing; do it and then move forward.

What can I do within the next 24 hours to go above and beyond what I would normally do?

____

____

____

____

Never stop envisioning your next step

Often when we reach a goal or an objective, we settle. Instead, once you reach your goal, set yourself up with an even bigger goal. Business, like life, is an evolution. It is a constant evolution of movements and a set of steps to get you to the next level. There is always a next step. Never stop working, and never stop evolving. By doing that, you will see the growth that you can achieve. You will feel the sense of accomplishment, but you will also feel the excitement of what is next.

Based on what you've accomplished this week, define your next step:

____

____

____

____

Don't let your goals disappear

We give up all the time. We get ideas and inspiration, write them down, and a few weeks later, it's like they never existed. By not letting your goals disappear, you remind yourself constantly not to let go of the prize. If you get an idea, write it down and analyze the feasibility of the idea. How will I execute this idea? Does this idea align with my goals and objectives? Does it get me closer to the ultimate goal of my life or my week or my month? If the answer is "yes" to all these questions, then embark on a new journey, and be relentless. Never give up if you know that you are working toward something. Some of our goals are not necessarily physical; they are spiritual goals, family goals, or relationship goals. What is important is not to let them disappear. We have too many distractions that can take us away from the prize. Will you be one of 99 percent that give up half-way or will you be one percent of the population that actually has a goal, carries it out, and fulfills that goal?

What is your goal this year? ______________________

____

____

To remember my goal, I will:

1. ____
2. ____
3. ____

Post it around your house, share it with people, and create affirmations.

Reward yourself for every step you achieve toward your goal!

Learn not to conform

Mediocrity is learning to conform; you defeat mediocrity with excellence. Don't get comfortable, instead, it is important to challenge yourself constantly. We conform with what is given to us; we conform to our circumstances. Some people say, "This is what I was given in my life, and I cannot do anything else." You are the driver of your own life, and you can change. You can learn not to conform, make it better, and challenge yourself.

You control what happens to you by the way that you react. There is no longer a circumstance, an event, or a person that is going to dictate how you feel and what you do with your life. Learn and apply excellence in everything you do because that is how you choose to react.

Think of one situation in your life that you can change or improve. What can you do today to demonstrate excellence in your life?

____

____

____

____

You are the driver of your life.

Apply the Law of Attraction

You can apply the Law of Attraction in your everyday life. Think about what you have now, the things you take for granted, and the things you don't appreciate on a daily basis, such as a warm bath, a home, a vehicle, a family, and a TV. Write down all the things you have now and be grateful for what you have. We are all made up of energy, thoughts, feelings and gratitude, so how we apply the Law of Attraction to our lives is the key. Ask. Believe. Receive. What do you want? Why do you want it? Be open to receive it.

Figure out what you want, believe that you already have it, and be open to receive it.

Success comes with responsibility

Taking care of clients, family, and businesses means many people are depending on you. It is hard to be the person that everybody expects you to be. You may get tired, or sick. It is hard sometimes to brave that responsibility, but you cannot be successful without being responsible. Recognize that success will come in the measure of your responsibility.

Do something out of the ordinary to get you closer to your goal this week.

Examples:
Get up earlier
Go to bed later
Don't watch TV

Use that time to continue to keep yourself on track for success!

Be willing to pay the price if you want to feel the reward and sense of accomplishment.

Do not let fear, indecision or doubt take over

Fear paralyzes you. Indecision influences you. Doubt does not allow you to move to the next step. These are the three reasons why people fail. How do you overcome the fear, the doubt, and the indecision? When I experience fear, I stop and think about why I am feeling that fear. I try to analyze the fear by listening to my inner self and looking at the situation objectively. Then I close my eyes, and I explode that fear in my mind. I watch that fear disintegrate before my eyes. After that, I realize that there's no reason to feel fear. This then allows me to make decisions to move forward without doubt.

Once you have listened to your intuition and analyzed your fear, consciously disintegrate the fear. Is there something holding you back today? What steps are you going to take to overcome that? If a family member is holding you back by saying you can't do something, what steps are you going to take to prove them wrong? Are you going to confront the person and say, "Stop doing this to me." Or are you just going to ignore it to move on?

What action are you going to take today so that you can start getting rid of those fears and doubts and instead reinforce yourself?

____

____

____

____

____

Success has its challenges

When your performance is mediocre, you are afraid of being criticized, afraid of failing, or afraid of losing your job. The common factor is fear. Frustration and anxiety can also get in the way. When you are successful, you have challenges as well. What if you do not succeed the next time? Either way, you have to choose whether you are going to stay this way or get better. If you conform with what you have and stay exactly where you are without the desire to grow and become better, stagnancy becomes a problem. About 95 percent of people are followers, and 5 percent are leaders. Be a leader and embrace the challenges of success.

List what you have to give up to be more successful, and list what you will get by giving up those things:

Give up...	*Will Get...*
____________________	____________________
____________________	____________________
____________________	____________________
____________________	____________________
____________________	____________________
____________________	____________________

Now take action.

Choose excellence

"Think only of the best, work only for the best, and expect only the best." This is part of the Optimist Creed by Christian D. Larson, and it signifies excellence. When you choose excellence, ownership is the outcome. You do your best when you own the process. We conform and think that half-way is good or doing something okay is good enough. We have every right to pursue excellence, to embrace excellence, and to be the best we can be.

For the next three days, live as though somebody is watching you at all times. Would you change anything that you are doing now?

☐ *Yes* ☐ *No*

If yes, what would that be?

___

___

___

172

Keep your health in mind

We are so busy coming and going that we often forget about our health. We underestimate our health, but it is critical to our success.

Make sure you take care of yourself. If you are not healthy, you cannot focus or do your best. Health is the vehicle that allows you to be your optimum self and execute as best you can.

Do one thing this week that puts your health first.

___

___

___

Repeat every week.

173

Recognize life's rewards- after challenges

Life often presents difficult situations personally and professionally. Sometimes you want to give up and not go on, but all of a sudden, you get a second wind. You continue on through the difficulty and don't give up. Life's rewards are sweet. People go through difficult situations and challenges, but just by hanging in there, you will be rewarded both personally and financially.

It's very important to recognize that life keeps presenting us with circumstances until we learn a lesson. If you are open to embrace those lessons, life gives you more to learn.

How did you turn a challenge into one of life's rewards?

What is one reward that you've gotten that you have not recognized until now?

____

____

____

174

Know when to take opportunities

We let opportunities pass us by. This is related to the Law of Attraction and the three-step process of achieving your goals: ask, believe, and receive. We do things and we ask for things, but then we are skeptical when opportunities present themselves. We lose many opportunities because we are skeptical about them being good for us. Stay focused. If you see an opportunity that you think will help you grow, you must take it. Know when to take good opportunities and when to let the bad ones pass you by.

Can you identify one opportunity that you can take this week to align with your passion?

____

____

____

Go above and beyond

Go the extra mile in everything you do. Do one more bit of research, take one more step, or add one more component. This helps you take your work to the next level, both as an individual and as a professional.

Going the extra mile will give you incredible rewards. In the Olympics and other major competitions, most of the time the main difference between first and second place, is a fraction of a second, but the prize is quite substantial. It is that fraction that sets the winner apart. Applying this mentally to your life can be very rewarding.

Choose one thing that you can do better this week:

___

___

___

Reward yourself for the process.

176

Affirmations work

Sometimes, we think our dreams are out of reach and simply not for us. Affirmations are great tools that remind you that you can achieve anything you want. They are usually written statements, or activities that give you the confidence to move forward. They must be stated in a positive way, in the present tense and with gratitude. For example, "I am grateful now that I am living a caffeine free life."

Use affirmations to create your own unique path, and stay focused.

Write down one goal that you have this month:

____

____

____

Post it where you can see it, and create an affirmation.

Download instructions for creating effective affirmations at: **www.bizsecretsthatwork.com/affirmations.pdf**

Visualize every day

We rely on what we see physically for our business to show us where we want to be and where we want to go. Visualization takes us to the place where we want to be (through our mind) so that you begin bringing about the steps to get there.

Focus on your inner guidance system, and visualize all the positive things that you want in your life. Through visualization, the physical manisfestation of your dreams will appear.

Do some research on visualization techniques.

Apply the one that resonates with you the most.

Outsource when needed

Do not own the chain of command; manage it. You do not need to have employees for every task. By outsourcing, you can get the best talent in a particular field. Because contractors or freelancers get paid on a per-project basis, you get people who are committed, who are good at what they do, and who are excited about making it happen for you. Minimize your risk and expense by outsourcing.

Write down one area of your business that you can outsource.

____

____

____

____

3 components to success

The three components for success, as given by my mentor, Jerry Mitchell, are:

1. **Passion**
2. **Timing**
3. **Integrity**

Yours might be different, depending on your industry, family situation, and other factors. But you must make sure you have a keen sense of awareness to recognize that you are at the right place and right time now. Use the ingredients of success that resonate with what you are trying to achieve in life, whether personally or professionally. That will give you the authenticity you need to be successful. Remember success for you is different than success for anybody else around you.

Define your own three components for success:

1 ____

2 ____

3 ____

180

Have a positive vision of success

We often envision failure. We focus mostly on the negative. I think it has a lot to do with the media and all that we see around us. This sets a tone for us in which we automatically default to the negative because that is what we see. What you see in your life now is what you have created in the past. What you see in the future is what you see in your mind today. That is why it is important to visualize success in a way that sets you apart from the negativity.

Visualize the outcome of something that you are going through that might be difficult.

Visualize a happy ending of a current difficulty.

Play that in your mind as many times as you can.

Recognize others' talents

Every person around you has talents that make them unique, but often go unnoticed. Whether it is cooking, speaking, dancing, or singing, we all have one or many talents.

Become the person that praises others, without expecting anything in return. If you recognize strengths in the people around you, you will also be recognized for your own.

Tell one individual this week what talent you see in him or her.

Who is that person?

___

What is his/her talent?

___

How will you help the person use that talent?

___

___

___

___

182

Surround yourself with positive people

Unfortunately, some of our family and friends may have negative attitudes. You receive your motivation and excitement from your surroundings, so make a conscious decision to surround yourself with people who have similar goals and objectives as yours. Identify people who are positive and who make you feel good when you speak with them. Find people who are smarter than you and who are positive, so when you are going through a difficult time in your life, you can count on them to help get you out of that negative circle and away from the people who may be dragging you down. You will be much more energized and motivated. Most importantly, you will have a support system when you need it.

Identify three positive people in your life.

1. ____
2. ____
3. ____

Stay in touch with them, and get energized!

Fill somebody else's cup

If you share your knowledge, your experiences, your love, and your passion, your cup is always going to be filled. When you help someone else, you are going to be helped as well. You give to receive. When you focus on helping other people, you will always be helped and there will always be someone to help you get to where you want to be.

One of my mentors, Brian Marshall, shared an interesting custom of living while visiting Japan. According to the Japanese culture, while eating dinner, it is up to you to fill the person's cup on your left throughout the meal. Because you are sitting to someone's left, your cup is always filled, too. This practice can be applied to everything in life.

Identify someone you can help this week. Completely out of the blue, just go up and say, "What can I do for you?"

Make people feel important

It does not matter whether you are the president or the school janitor. We all have a basic need to feel important, to be recognized, and to feel that we're making a contribution to the world. To help other people feel important, compliment them on the little things, whether it's the way they look or something they've done; keep in mind that you must be genuine. You will feel more confident about yourself and be happy that you affected somebody else's life!

Compliment at least three people this week.

It does not have to be something huge, but it must be genuine.

Breathe happiness

Life has many simple, happy things to offer. Recognizing those small things will propel you to embrace the big things.

A few years ago, I began to breathe happiness. Breathe happiness? Yes, that is correct! I don't have to have something extraordinary happening to experience this during the day. I simply stop for a moment, take a deep breath, remember a happy moment, and feel the bliss! It's that easy!

When you breathe happiness, you can re-energize yourself and attract more happiness to your life!

Take a deep breath.

Consciously breath in and out.

Feel and think of a moment that makes you happy.

Do it until it becomes a habit.

Read, learn, and apply new things

With so much information coming at us every day, it is hard at times to pinpoint a lesson to incorporate into your business. When I came to the United States, I was 14 years old and did not speak English. I made it a point to learn at least one or two new words every day. I would journal the words that stood out to me and write them 10 times. By doing this, I memorized the way the word was written, but my job was not done. The next day, I would ask my teacher how the word was pronounced, what it meant, and how to use it. Immediately, I began using the word and never forgot it. Be inquisitive about new things and ask questions.

What business lesson have I learned today?

____

____

____

____

Don't focus on your limitations

As a young, Latina woman, for the longest time, I believed my weaknesses would never allow me to get to where I wanted to be. One day, I realized that those perceived limitations were my greatest strengths. I decided that being a young Latina woman would give me an edge in my business. It has proven to be my most valuable asset as an entrepreneur. You, too, can turn your limitations into positive opportunities.

What do you consider your limitations, and how can you convert them to core competencies?

Create good habits

Good habits create a lifetime of success and a lifetime of positivity. Most things we do are habits. One great habit is going the extra mile. If you can stick to something for 21 days, you have created a habit. This is your lifestyle, the way you live your life, and part of who you are. When your habits are good, you have integrity.

Select one positive habit to create - *anything from arriving at work 15 minutes early, to exercising, or spending one hour a week reading about your industry.*

___

___

___

___

___

___

___

Do this for at least 21 days.

Your own GPS

You use your subconscious mind to generate feelings, and those feelings generate tangible things. I believe we all have our own inner-guidance system; we have our own GPS. We go outside and look for answers, but the answers are inside of us. You can tap into your subconscious mind for something positive and to create anything you want. Go to a quiet spot, and think about what you want to create for your life. Visualize yourself already in possession of that. Repeat this every night and every morning so you can see whatever it is you want in your life. Every morning and evening, read a written statement of what you want. Your built-in guidance system can give you everything that you desire.

Create a statement below.

____

____

____

____

____

____

____

____

Read it and visualize it day in and day out.

Have "think-tank" sessions regularly

We're so inundated with tasks on a daily basis that we forget to stop and think. We lose sight and we lose objectiveness. Our lives are built on habit, and what we do on a regular basis does not require a lot of thinking. Having think-tank sessions allows you and your team to develop ways to improve and come up with new creative ideas. You can achieve more with less time; you can maximize your opportunities.

For the next month, schedule a think-tank session at least once a week.

191

Assume responsibility

Assuming responsibility is not necessarily a negative experience; it can be a very positive experience because you are standing up and saying, "I did this." One simple way of assuming responsibility is when somebody gives you an assignment, turn to them and say, "This is what you have told me I am going to do, this is the result that you want, and this is the time by which you need it done." Then go the extra mile to get it done faster, and say, "This is what you asked me to do, this is where I am, these are the issues that I have solved, and here is my next step." You will create opportunities for success by taking ownership of your projects and your clients' success.

Create the habit of taking responsibility.

"Today I am enjoying accepting responsibility. I am accepting responsibility for what I think, what I feel, what I say, and what I do. I am moving forward positively toward the direction in which I want my life to go."

Do it!

Keep at it

Many times, we start something and then never finish. This is the difference between achieving our goals and not achieving them. By keeping yourself focused on the one thing you want to accomplish, you can make incredible things come to life that you could never have imagined. Break it down and establish structure and discipline. Set a time limit for finishing your project, and get it done. Keeping at it always makes a difference.

Select one thing you want to accomplish and apply the following steps:

Step one: *break it down*
Step two: *create a structure*
Step three: *apply the discipline*

Control your thoughts

We have more than 60,000 thoughts a day—thoughts we can't control because there are so many of them and they come from so many different directions. Some are positive, and some are negative. If you can control your thoughts, you can stay at the optimum level all the time. One way to control your thoughts is through your feelings. Think about things that make you feel good, and all of a sudden, that negative thought is gone. You can turn a negative thought into something positive immediately just by doing something that makes you feel good.

Monitor how you feel, be aware of your feelings, and have something such as a quote, a piece of inspiration, or a memory that can change the way you feel.

194

Do it now

We always say we will do something tomorrow. Tomorrow I am going to start exercising; tomorrow I am going to start calling people. Why are you waiting for tomorrow? Do it now. Once you establish your priorities, start working on them, and get them done. Feel the sense of accomplishment from scratching tasks off your list.

Pick one secret in this book and do it NOW, without hesitation.

What secret will you apply now?

Secret #: ____________________

Brace for impact

Every decision we make has an impact, small or large. The "Law of Cause and Effect" takes place whether we want it to or not. Based on the magnitude of the decision, it might have a short-term effect that disappears immediately or a long-term effect that lasts a lifetime. Education, for example, has a sustainable impact for a lifetime. Being aware of the impact, will help you take a proactive approach.

Write down a decision you are contemplating:

____

____

____

Analyze three possible outcomes of this decision:

____

____

____

196

Passion chases you down

LaMeisha Taylor, one of the most passionate people I know, once told me that, "There is no real success without passion." She is a driven, motivated, and extremely positive individual. LaMiesha has gone through some major difficulties in her life, but that does not stop her from shining a light of positivity around the people she comes in contact with. No matter what happens to you, passion will put you back on track!

Passion...
Opens doors
Infuses your creativity
Increases your capacity
Provides financial reward

Use the rectangular space below to write down all the things that you are passionate about (no limitations; use a bigger piece of paper if you need it):

How can you use your passion this week to create positivity around you? *(If your passion is painting, do a piece of art and give it to someone you appreciate.)*

___

___

___

Sushisa Vereshet

The phrase is not English, Spanish, or Chinese. I am not really sure what language it is, but a kind woman gave me a postcard with the phrase and a picture of a tree that had been cut down and was almost completely dried. A blossom of life was right in the center.

I was going through a very difficult time in my life and she told me to remember that phrase "Sushisa Vereshet." I have gone through many more life challenges, but this simple postcard reminds me that I can get back on track. No matter what difficulty you face in life, you can blossom again and again.

What inspiration keeps you going during difficult times?

☐ *Phrase or quote*
☐ *Card*
☐ *Stone*
☐ *Journal*
☐ *Book*
☐ *Other:* ______________________________

If you don't have one, create it this week.

198

Use third-party tools

Third-party tools are incredible for self-development. Third-party tools include books, CDs, DVDs, white papers, articles, presentations, etc. They are extremely powerful because they are non-biased and are provided to a captive audience. I started reading when I was four years old, and soon after that my mother started introducing me to third-party tools. Oftentimes, when I think about my childhood, I think of Zig Ziglar, Napoleon Hill, Dale Carnegie, Og Mandino, and many others. Every time my mom took me to a motivational seminar, I would ask her to stay until almost everyone left so that I could greet the speakers and shake their hand. I hoped that someday, I would be like one of them. I have incorporated those early childhood teachings into my daily life.

It is never too late to introduce third-party tools. The more you are exposed to positive information, the more you will make it part of your life and succeed!

This week, perform one of the following:

☐ Read 10 pages of a good book

☐ Listen for 15 minutes to a good tape

☐ Read 1 article or white paper

☐ Attend a self-development seminar

It's all about self-development!

199

Make it happen!

So many people give up before the challenge begins. We all have great ideas in our heads, but most of us don't do anything with them. Michelangelo once said,***"I saw the angel in the marble and carved until I set him free."*** It is the favorite quote of my mastermind partner Chris Beebe.

This quote is the essence of turning something non-existent, such as an idea, a dream, or a goal, into its physical manifestation. No matter how big or small your goal is, by creating it in your mind and taking the steps to get there, you are a winner. It doesn't matter if it takes you one day, one year, or a lifetime; making it happen is what matters in the end.

I am committed to turning ideas into physical manifestations, and one of my mottos has become: "Make it happen!" In fact, I love making things happen so much that I even gave myself the title of "Make-It-Happen Director," instead of CEO or President of my marketing/PR agency. As we engage new clients and they see the title, they are confident that I am committed to their success because I like to make things happen. By having a make-it-happen attitude, you will turn all your dreams into a reality.

Take a step towards one goal you have this week.

Just make it happen!

What is your secret?

There are 199 secrets in this book. *The secret "200" is all about you!*

Use this space to write down your own secret to success.

My secret:

____

____

____

Why is it important?

____

____

____

How do "I" do it?

____

____

____

What is the happy ending of using this secret?

____

____

____

Share it online at **www.bizsecretsthatwork.com/mysecret**

Forms

The following forms are incredible tools to help you navigate the journey to success.

Download them free of charge!

Who are you? .... *www.bizseretsthatwork.com/whoareyou.pdf*

Setting Goals .... *www.bizsecretsthatwork.com/goals.pdf*

Balanced Life .... *www.bizsecretsthatwork.com/balance.pdf*

Affirmation Steps ...... *www.bizsecretsthatwork.com/affirmations.pdf*

SWOT Analysis .... *www.bizsecretsthatwork.com/swot.pdf*

Marketing Mix .... *www.bizsecretsthatwork.com/mktmix.pdf*

Sales Funnel ....*www.bizsecretsthatwork.com/funnel.pdf*

Marketing Calendar .*www.bizsecretsthatwork.com/mktcalendar.pdf*

Referral Machine *www.bizsecretsthatwork.com/referralmachine.pdf*

Mind Mapping .... *www.bizsecretsthatwork.com/mindmapping.pdf*

Resources

Carnegie, Dale. *How to Win Friends and Influence People. Simon and Schuster, New York, NY 1936*

Hill, Napoleon. *Think and Grow Rich. Fawcett Publications, Greenwich, TN 1960*

Byrne, Rhonda. *The Secret. Atria Books/Beyond Words 2008*

Covey, Steven. *The 7 Habits of Highly Effective People. Free Press, New York, NY 1989*

Ogilvy, Dave. *Oglivy on Advertising. Crown Publishers, USA 1983*

Bobbinski, Dan. *Passion Driven Teams. Career Press, Franklin Lakes, NJ 2009*

Beckwith, Harry. *Selling the Invisible. Warner Books, NY 1997*

Gordon, Jon. *The Energy Bus: 10 Rules to Fuel Your Life, Work and Team with Positive Energy. John Wiley and Sons, NJ 2007*

Collins, Jim. *Good to Great. Harper Collins Publishers, NY 2001*

Eisenberg, Brian. *Call to Action. Thomas Nelson, TN 2006*

About the Author

Born in Mexico City, Jacqueline Camacho-Ruiz moved to the United States at age 14, where she learned English in just one year and put herself through college. Upon graduating college, she launched what is it now the award-winning JJR Marketing Consultants agency in Illinois.
(To learn more visit: www.jjrmarketing.com).

Wanting to share her secrets for success with others, Camacho-Ruiz penned this easy-to-follow "how-to" book to encourage other business professionals in the areas of sales, marketing, and customer retention. Motivating and inspiring, the book also features critical success secrets for anyone starting a business.

Camacho-Ruiz has based her life on the philosophy that the gift comes in the giving. On any day, you will find her graciously giving more than she receives. This book is no different.

Jaqueline was recognized as an Emerging Leader by the Chicago Association of Direct Marketing, received the "Entrepreneurial Excellence Award" by The Business Ledger and was one of two finalists for the "Latina Entrepreneur of the Year" by Chicago Latino Network. She is a regular guest host on Livin' the Dream Radio Show and the Spanish newspaper editorial columnist for Ultimas Noticias. She also contributes to several local and national publications.

CPSIA information can be obtained at www.ICGtesting.com
264984BV00005B/1/P